Pizza

50 Traditional and Alternative
Recipes for the Oven and Grill

Pizza

Dwayne Ridgaway

QUARRY BOOKS

First published in the United States of America by:
Quarry Books, an imprint of
Rockport Publishers, Inc.
33 Commercial Street
Gloucester, Massachusetts 01930-5089
Telephone: (978) 282-9590
Fax: (978) 283-2742
www.rockpub.com

Library of Congress Cataloging-in-Publication Data
Ridgaway, Dwayne.
    Pizza : 50 traditional and alternative recipes for the oven and grill / Dwayne
Ridgaway.
        p.   cm.
    Includes index.
    ISBN 1-59253-154-7 (pb)
    1. Pizza. [1. Cookery.] I. Title.
TX770.P58R54 2005
    641.8′248—dc22   2004025592
                                    CIP

ISBN 1-59253-154-7

10 9 8 7 6 5 4 3 2 1

Design: Wilson Harvey, London
Cover Image and Photography: Allan Penn Photography

Printed in Singapore

To Shelby, my dearest friend in heaven

Family and friends make these projects possible through love and encouragement. Without singling out any one, I dedicate this to them all—they know who they are.

Thank you all!

Contents

Introduction
A brief history of pizza 8

Chapter 1
**Ingredients: Traditional and
Not So Traditional 10**
Dough Ingredients 11
Toppings 13

Chapter 2
The Basics 16
Sauces and Spreads 17
    Basic Tomato Sauce 17
    Spicy Tomato Sauce 18
    Proven Basil Pesto 20
Dough Recipes 22
    Basic Pizza Dough 22
    No-Oil Neapolitan-Style
       Pizza Dough 24
    Whole Wheat and Honey
       Pizza Dough 25
    Herbed Pizza Dough 26
    Chocolate Pizza Dough 28
    Sweet Pizza Dough 29
    Dark Beer Crust 30
    Basil Pesto Pizza Dough 31
    Pizza Dough Alternatives 32
Other Basic Ingredients 33
    Oven-Dried Tomatoes 33
    Roasted Peppers 33
    Roasted Garlic 33

Chapter 3
Cooking Tools and Techniques 34
Cooking Techniques 35
    Oven Baking 35
    Grilling 35
    Gas Grilling 35
    Wood and Charcoal Grilling 36
Appliances 37

Chapter 4
Classic Pizza 38

Pizza Margherita 39
Spinach-Stuffed Pizza 40
BBQ Chicken Pizza with Smoked
 Gouda and Grilled Pineapples 43
Meatball and Tomato Stew
 Grilled Pizza 44
Wood-Grilled Chicken Pizza
 with Radicchio and Feta 46
Caramelized Leek and Golden
 Potato Grilled Pizza 48
Cheesiest Cheesy
 and Herb Pizza 49
Roasted Wild Mushroom Pizza
 with Pancetta and Feta 50
Garlic-Grilled Chicken and Pepperoni
 Pizza with Smoked Gouda 52
New York–Style Stone-
 Baked Pizza 54
Grilled Asparagus and Cheese
 Pizza with White Truffle Oil 56
Individual Grilled Greek-
 Style Pizza 58
Pesto and Black Olive Pizza 60
Chicago-Style Deep-Dish Pizza 62
Pizza Bianca with Roasted Garlic,
 Ricotta, and Broccoli Rabe 64
Deli Counter Calzone 66
Ziti Pizza with Citrus Chicken
 and Mozzarella 68
Clam and Roasted Garlic Thin-
 Crust Pizza 69

Chapter 5
Contemporary Pizza 70

Buffalo Chicken Stuffed-Skillet
 Pizza 72
Brunch Pizza with Scrambled
 Eggs and Tasso Ham 74
Western Omelet Grilled Pizza 76
Tenderloin and Portobello
 Mushroom Pizza with
 Roasted Garlic 77
Thai Chicken Pizza 78
Pizza with Rosemary Shrimp
 and Spicy Golden Potatoes 80
Grilled Hoisin Chicken Pizza 82
Teriyaki Shrimp Grilled Pizza 84
Shitake Mushroom Breakfast
 Pizza 86
Ciabatta Pizza Loaves 88
Bloody Mary Shrimp Pizza with
 Fried Garlic 90
Marinara and Mozzarella Pizza
 with Stuffed Crust 92
German Sausage and Sauerkraut
 Pizza with Dark Beer Crust 93
Hummus and Grilled Eggplant
 Pizza with Feta and Oven-Dried
 Tomatoes 94
Hors d'oeuvres Lavash Pizzas 96
 *Pear and Gorgonzola with
  Tarragon 98*
 Prosciutto and Basil 98
 *Caramelized Onion and
  Rosemary with Pancetta 99*
 Pesto, Olive, and Goat Cheese 99
Pizza Montréal 100
Grilled Pizza with Fried Calamari 101
Black Bean and Roasted Corn
 Pizza with Seared Shrimp and
 Monchego Cheese 102

Chapter 6
Salad Pizzas 104

Chicken Caesar Salad Pizza 106
Fontina and Gruyere Pizza with
 Skirt Steak Salad 108
Ancho-Seared Shrimp and
 Spicy Caesar Pizza 110
Grilled Vegetable Salad Pizza with
 Parmesan Balsamic Vinaigrette 112
Asian Salad Grilled Pizza 114

Chapter 7
Sweet Pizzas 116

Mixed Berries on Grilled Pizza
 Shell with Mascarpone
 Spread 116
Apple Crumble "Pizza" 119
Apricot and Blackberry Pizza
 with Camembert and Sweet
 Ricotta Cheese 120
Grilled Strawberry and Mango
 Chocolate Pizza 122

Index 125
Acknowledgments 127
About the Author 128

Introduction

Around the world, pizza may be the most recognized and most consumed food ever. And, as its popularity continues to grow, more and more people make pizza at home. Homemade pizza is fun and easy to assemble, is more delicious than home delivered, and offers ample opportunity for experienced and beginner cooks alike to make a healthy, satisfying meal.

While many people consider pizza an old-world Italian phenomenon, it is actually the product of many ancient cultures centered around the Mediterranean Sea. It appears to have evolved from many cultures, including Ancient Greece, Rome, and Egypt. The Greeks ate *plankuntos*, a flat baked bread with assorted toppings that probably derived from the Babylonians centuries before them. In ancient Egypt, historical accounts indicate that the Pharaoh's birthday was celebrated by eating a flat bread seasoned with herbs. And from early Rome came the word *picea*, possibly the root of the word pizza, which translates as "the blackening of bread in an oven."

The modern pizza probably evolved from pre-Renaissance Naples, Italy. A large city in the center of Italy, Naples has been at the forefront of culinary evolution for centuries.

Largely believed to be peasant food, pizza ironically became a royal delight in Naples in 1889, when Rafaele Esposito of the *Pizzeria di Pietro e Basta Cosi* (now known as *Pizzeria Brandi*) served a pizza as a tribute to the visiting King Umberto I and Queen Margherita. Rafaele topped flat dough with fresh basil, tomatoes, and buffalo mozzarella, very fittingly representing the three colors of the Italian flag. The king and queen adored the pizza, and so was born Pizza Margherita.

Naples is also the home of brick-oven pizza and, as such, has heavily influenced the dough, ingredients, and cooking techniques used by many New York pizzerias today. The tradition of Neapolitan pizza is so revered, in fact, that the *Associazione Verace Pizza Napoletana* (the Association of True Neapolitan Pizza) regulates what is and who can make true Neapolitan pizza.

Pizza made its debut on American soil with the influx of Italian immigrants in the latter half of the nineteenth century. By the turn of the century, Italians had begun opening their own bakeries and groceries in the streets of New York, selling pizza alongside bread and other produce. It wasn't until the end of World War II, however, when returning GIs created a nationwide demand for pizza, that it became a bona fide staple in American eateries.

During the last 60 years, Americans have topped the flat, white dough with their own combinations of ingredients and flavors. Today, there are three well-defined styles of pizza in the United States: New York–style, viewed as the direct descendant of Italian pizza; Chicago-style, a thick-crust pizza, which is often stuffed; and California-style, which marries a thin crust with new-world ingredients and flavors. Grilled pizza is the newest entry in the pages of pizza history. This smoky, robust pizza may have originated in Providence, Rhode Island.

Travel the United States from one coast to the other, and you will experience more styles and flavors of pizza than could ever be compiled in one volume. In this book, I have included recipes that explore the classics, pairing ingredients and dough recipes directly from old-world methods, as well as more modern recipes that marry new and innovative flavors and cooking techniques.

When making any pizza, be creative: Let the ingredients you have on hand and the flavors you like influence what you make. The recipes here can be enjoyed as is, or altered to fit your personal taste. Throughout this book, the cooking techniques, ingredients, and toppings for pizza are interchangeable for all recipes. Grilling one instead of oven-baking it, or taking a topping from one recipe and adding it to another is always an option. Creativity is what brought pizza across the Atlantic Ocean and made it the American icon that it is today, so celebrate the endless possibilities that this classic meal offers the home cook.

chapter 1

Ingredients: Traditional and Not So Traditional

Dough Ingredients

[Flour]

A pizza crust achieves its prominent characteristics—texture, tenderness, and pliability—in large part from the type of flour you use. Quite simply, the higher the protein level in a flour, the greater the formation of gluten. As the dough is kneaded, the gluten forms into sheets, which trap the gas released by the yeast and the air produced by kneading. With high-protein flour, the gluten strands are strong enough to prevent the gas and air from escaping, which creates a thicker crust. Low-protein flours, on the other hand, typically produce baked goods with little to no trapped gas and air, making them flatter (and more tender). A low-protein flour (with less gluten) will produce a softer, more tender dough; a high-protein flour (with more gluten), like all-purpose flour, will produce a dense and chewy dough.

Pizzas from different regions are often defined by the style or texture of the crust, which is a direct result of the type of flour used in that region. Italian pizza, specifically Neapolitan pizza, for instance, is known for its soft and tender thin crust. This type of pizza crust is made with a finely milled flour from winter wheat that is low in gluten. Soft winter wheat is also used to mill American cake flour and southern all-purpose flour, both of which produce a tender texture in baked goods. To emulate a traditional Neapolitan crust, look for authentic imported Italian flour, or use cake flour combined with unbleached all-purpose flour (see the recipe for No-Oil Neapolitan-Style Pizza Dough on page 24.)

To achieve a firmer, stretchable dough, as found in New York pizzerias, choose bread flour, which is high in protein and produces a high rise. Like bread flour, semolina, a flour used in pasta, is high in protein and takes longer to rise. If using semolina, you may need more water than is called for with an all-purpose or cake-flour crust. Crusts made with bread flour and semolina can be stretched very thin and are perfect for grilling.

Self-rising flour is a variety of flour with added baking powder and salt. This type of flour is great for quick-rising doughs, such as the Basic Pizza Dough on page 22.

Most home cooks will have one flour on hand—unbleached all-purpose flour—and that works fine for pizza making at home. All-purpose flour produces a great dough, somewhere between thin and crisp and dense and chewy.

One note about the flour amounts called for in this book's recipes: The amount of flour suggested is just that—a suggestion; determining how much flour to use is not an exact science. The consistency of dough can vary according to water type (tap vs. bottled, hard vs. soft) or the humidity, temperature, and altitude of your location. When making and kneading dough, you may need more or less flour, but be sure to add the flour in small amounts. Too much flour, and your crust may turn out tough.

[Yeast]

Yeast is most commonly known as the rising agent in pizza dough, but it can also be considered the heart of dough

110°F to 115°F (43°C–46°C). This is important because water that is too hot or too cold will kill the yeast. Use an ordinary candy or meat thermometer to determine the accurate temperature.

[Oils]

Olive oil is a staple in pizza making, although it is not typically used in Neapolitan (New York–style) dough. I like the intensity it adds to the flavor of dough as well as the smooth texture it imparts.

Olive oil varies according to the method in which it was produced. Products labeled simply "olive oil" are made from the second and third pressings of the olives, which produces a light-colored oil with a less-intense flavor at a reasonable retail cost. This variety of olive oil is great for everyday cooking and pizza making. I prefer extra-virgin olive oil for its richer, more intense flavor when the dough recipe calls for oil or to drizzle on top of a finished pie. While better olive oil is slightly more expensive, it is worth it for the flavor.

Today, the oil section of your local supermarket is almost as large as the produce department. There are no hard and fast rules here—try experimenting with sesame, peanut, walnut, hazelnut, or chili oils; each will add its own unique flavor to your pizzas.

making. Yeast is a living organism that, when brought to life in warm water, begins a feeding frenzy on the elements around it; this in turn causes the dough to rise. Think of rising time as the time when the dough develops flavor. The longer the rising time, the greater the flavor. The first rise usually takes place in an oiled bowl, covered with plastic wrap or a clean kitchen towel, in a warm, dry place. This setup shortens the rising time. If time permits, allowing your dough to rise more slowly, such as overnight in the refrigerator, can intensify the flavors. If you let your dough rise in the refrigerator, be sure to let it come to room temperature before stretching and/or working it.

[Water]

Water is an integral part of the pizza dough–making process. Many people may not realize that the water you use has a big impact on the dough. If the water in your area has high levels of chlorine or fluoride, for instance, you should use filtered water or store-bought purified water instead. The added chemicals in tap water can affect the development of the yeast as well as the flavor of the dough. (I once heard of a pizza shop in California that buys its water from Brooklyn, New York, to ensure an authentic New York–style crust!)

Reactivating the yeast in warm water is critical to the creation of the dough. All of the dough recipes in this book call for water with a temperature of

Toppings

[Cheese]

In the minds of some, pizza without cheese isn't pizza at all. For pizza makers, there are literally hundreds of cheeses, offering a wide variety of flavors and textures, to choose from. If you are unsure of the flavor of a specific cheese, ask your store clerk or deli counter attendant for help. While I encourage experimentation, not all cheeses are appropriate for pizza making. Here are a few simple rules to keep in mind:

- **Melting** If possible, select a cheese that melts well (and becomes stringy and gooey) in heat. While some recipes call for goat or feta cheese (which do not melt well) as a topping, these are usually final additions to the pizza, where they brown and keep their shape and texture.
- **Flavor** In general, use a mild-flavored cheese, if the flavors of the other ingredients are strong, and a sharp or more pungent cheese, if the other ingredients are mellow or mild in flavor. Of course, there are no hard-and-fast rules regarding this subject; in the end, it's a matter of personal taste.
- **Quantity** For some people, there can never be too much cheese on a pizza. If you are making a thin-crust pizza, however, too much cheese can make the crust soggy and flimsy. If you're making a thick-crust pizza, on the other hand, you should add enough cheese to balance the weight and/or flavors of the other ingredients.

The most common type of cheese used on pizza is mozzarella. Italian pizzas typically use mozzarella cheese made from the milk of the water buffalo. Introduced to Italy in the seventeenth century from India, buffalo mozzarella is, like tomatoes, a staple in classic pizza making.

In this country, buffalo mozzarella can be found packed in water at your supermarket's deli counter. If you really want to make traditional Pizza Margherita, it's worth the effort to track some down. Your deli may also sell other types of fresh mozzarella, and these also work well. The more popular, and usually more readily available, type of mozzarella cheese is cow's-milk mozzarella, which is made from whole or skim milk and packed in plastic. This variety usually has less flavor than fresh and may become stringy when baked, but it is perfectly adequate if you can't find fresh mozzarella.

Provolone is another popular cheese for pizza making. Provolone is a pungent cheese that ranges from mild to sharp, just as cheddar cheese does. It is usually available at the deli counter, sliced to order, or in the gourmet cheese section of your supermarket.

Parmesan cheese and Pecorino Romano are used for dusting the pizza crust before adding toppings or to finish off a stuffed crust. The most recognizable grated Parmesan cheese comes in a green shaker can, but fresh varieties are available in just about every supermarket and taste dramatically better. Parmesan cheese is made all over the world, but there is only one Parmigiano-Reggiano, which has been made in Italy the same way for more than

700 years. The production of Parmigiano-Regiano is strictly controlled to ensure its authentic characteristics and taste. Pecorino Romano is also a very popular grated cheese. Made from sheep's milk, Romano is a robust, semihard cheese with a granular texture.

[Tomatoes]

Tomatoes were introduced to Italy by the Spaniards, who had discovered them in Peru and Mexico. At first, they were considered poisonous, but later their true virtues were discovered. Today, tomatoes are an integral part of pizza making.

Whether using in a sauce or as a fresh topping, always insist on the highest-quality canned product or firm, beautifully ripe, fresh tomatoes. Short of growing them yourself, try to find a farmstand or market in your area that offers the freshest tomatoes.

Here are a few important notes to keep in mind. If you plan to top your pizza with sliced fresh tomatoes, I recommend using a thicker crust. When baked, tomatoes release a great deal of moisture, which can make your crust soggy and flimsy. For oven drying, the Roma or plum variety of tomato is best, as their size and moisture content work well in the oven. When using canned tomatoes, find good-quality Italian products. There is no reason not to use canned tomatoes; just look for those with the fewest preservatives or added ingredients.

[Herbs]

Most of the recipes throughout this book call for fresh herbs. There is no substitute for the intense flavor and color of fresh herbs. Basil, parsley, thyme, chives, cilantro, mint, rosemary, and tarragon are the most common herbs I use in pizza making. As with tomatoes, it's worth the effort to find a market that sells fresh, quality herbs, or you can grow your own very easily for very little money. Although dried herbs will suffice in a pinch, your pizza will taste significantly better if you use fresh herbs. There is one exception: The Herbed Pizza Dough recipe (page 26) calls for dried herbs because they can stand up to the heat of the oven.

[Vegetables]

Pizza is basically a blank canvas on which you can combine your favorite toppings to create a masterpiece. Vegetables are an important part of the masterpiece. Whether grilled, sautéed, roasted, or fresh, vegetables have a tremendous flavor and texture impact on pizza. As with cheese, don't be afraid to experiment.

Here are a few pointers to keep in mind. Fresh vegetables, depending on their size, take longer to cook than most other ingredients. Firm varieties such as squash, asparagus, onions, peppers, and broccoli take much longer to cook than it will take for your cheese to melt. I recommend blanching them in boiling water, or sautéing or grilling them before using them on your pizza. Tender vegetables, like mushrooms and leafy greens, on the other hand, don't need much time to cook. They can also release a large amount of moisture, however, which may make your crust soggy. For this reason, I recommend cooking them briefly before use.

chapter 2

The Basics

[sauces and spreads]

There are three very basic elements to pizza making: dough, sauce, and toppings. Toppings may include cheese, vegetables, meats, and herbs. This chapter contains very basic recipes to get you started on the path to making great pizza at home. Later chapters will include more creative variations and ideas.

2 (28-ounce [795 g]) cans best-quality peeled plum tomatoes with juice

4 cloves garlic, peeled and coarsely chopped

1 tablespoon (18 g) coarse salt

1 tablespoon (15 g) sugar

1/3 cup (75 ml) extra-virgin olive oil

1 cup (30 g) loosely packed fresh basil leaves

2 tablespoons (30 g) tomato paste

1/4 teaspoon (0.5 g) black pepper

2 teaspoons (2.5 g) dried oregano

1/4 cup (60 ml) red wine

Place all the ingredients in a large sauce pot. Bring to a boil, then stir and boil for about 5 minutes, crushing the tomatoes with the back of a spoon while stirring. Reduce heat and simmer for 20 minutes, stirring occasionally. Use immediately, or refrigerate for up to 5 days. This sauce can be made, chilled, and then frozen in airtight containers for up to 3 months.

[Makes 4 cups (950 ml)]

Basic Tomato Sauce

This sauce was originally developed for use in lasagna, but it also makes a great pizza sauce. Quick and tasty, this tomato sauce takes very little prep (you don't even have to chop the basil) and cooking time. The trick is to use fresh basil. I do not recommend substituting dried basil.

¼ cup (60 ml) olive oil

1 medium yellow onion, finely chopped

4 garlic cloves, minced

1 teaspoon (1.3 g) crushed red pepper flakes

¼ teaspoon (0.5 g) cayenne pepper

¾ cup (175 ml) dry red wine

2 (28-ounce [795 g]) cans whole peeled tomatoes

1 (28-ounce [795 g]) can tomato sauce

1 tablespoon (15 g) tomato paste

1 tablespoon (4 g) minced fresh oregano

⅓ cup (20 g) packed fresh basil leaves, roughly torn

½ teaspoon (0.5 g) minced fresh thyme

2 teaspoons (10 g) sugar

2 tablespoons (10 g) freshly grated Parmesan cheese

Salt and freshly ground black pepper to taste

In a large stock pot, heat the olive oil over medium-high heat; add onion, garlic, red pepper flakes, and cayenne pepper, and sauté until onions are just tender, about 3 minutes. Add red wine, stir, and reduce by half, then add the canned tomatoes, crushing with hands. Add tomato sauce and tomato paste and combine. Bring to a boil, then reduce heat to low; add oregano, basil, and thyme, and simmer for 30 minutes, stirring occasionally. Stir in sugar and Parmesan cheese, and cook for an additional 15 minutes. Season with salt and black pepper. Use immediately, or cool completely and refrigerate for up to 1 week. The sauce may also be frozen: once it is completely cool, place in airtight bags or containers, and freeze for up to 2 months.

[Makes 4 cups (950 ml)]

Spicy Tomato Sauce

Red pepper flakes and ground red pepper give this sauce a bit of a kick. The long simmering time allows the flavors to intensify the sauce.

FOR THE PROCESSOR:

2 cups (120 g) tightly packed fresh basil leaves

1/2 cup (120 ml) extra virgin olive oil

1/2 cup (68 g) pine nuts

4 garlic cloves, chopped fine

Salt

FOR COMPLETION BY HAND:

1/2 cup (40 g) freshly grated Parmigiano-Reggiano cheese

2 tablespoons (10 g) freshly grated Romano cheese

3 tablespoons (45 g) butter softened to room temperature

Proven Basil Pesto

Basil pesto, with its vibrant green color and tremendous flavor, is a staple in Italian cooking. It is as rich in history as it is in taste. Originally pesto was created by the Genoese to celebrate the exceptional flavor of a fresh harvest.

Italian culinary tradition calls for hand blending pesto by the old-world mortar and pestle method. The Italians might be correct linguistically, because the word pesto derives from the verb *pestare*, which translates "to pound" or "to grind," as in the method of using a mortar. However, making pesto this way is time consuming, and requires special equipment, so most modern cooks use a food processor for the initial blending. For a great finished texture, however, I recommend mixing in the cheeses and butter by hand.

Briefly soak and wash the basil in cold water, then gently pat it dry using paper towels. Place the basil, pine nuts, chopped garlic, and an ample pinch of salt in the bowl of the processor fitted with the blade attachment, then process for a few seconds. Add the olive oil, scrape down the sides of the bowl, and continue processing until uniform and creamy. Transfer to a bowl, and mix in the Parmigiano-Reggiano and Romano cheeses by hand. Once the cheese is evenly incorporated, mix in the butter, distributing it uniformly into the sauce. Use the pesto immediately or refrigerate in an airtight container for up to 5 days. After refrigeration, allow the sauce to warm to room temperature before using.

[A note on cheese]
Classic pesto is made with the pecorino cheese known as *fiore sardo*, which has a milder flavor than Romano. If using *fiore sardo* in this recipe, reduce the Parmigiano-Reggiano to between 2 tablespoons (10 g) and replace Romano with ½ cup (40 g) *fiore sardo*.

[Freezing pesto]
If you plan on freezing your pesto, blend it in the food processor, stopping before adding the cheeses and butter. When ready to use, thaw completely, then mix in the cheese and butter by hand just before using. Pesto can be frozen in an airtight container for several months. In summer, fresh basil is plentiful, so many home cooks make several batches of pesto and freeze it for use in the fall and winter months.

[Makes 1 large 16- to 18-inch (41 – 46 cm) pizza or two traditional deep-dish pizzas]

Basic Pizza Dough

After testing numerous pizza dough recipes, I arrived at this, my favorite basic pizza dough. The consistency and texture is similar to that of traditional deep-dish pizza, but this is a great all-purpose dough that works well for all recipes. Follow each individual pizza recipe carefully for exact dough requirements.

1 1/2 cups (355 ml) warm water
(about 110˚F to 115˚F [43˚C – 46˚C])

1 (1/4-ounce [7 g]) package
active dry yeast

1 teaspoon (5 g) sugar

3 1/2 cups (385 g) all-purpose flour

1/2 cup (38 g) semolina flour
(or fine ground yellow corn meal)

1/3 cup (75 ml) olive oil, plus
extra for brushing bowl

1 teaspoon (5 g) salt

Combine the water, yeast, and sugar in a large mixing bowl, then stir to combine and dissolve the yeast. Set aside until foamy on top, about 5 minutes. Add 1 1/2 cups (165 g) flour, the semolina, 1/3 cup (75 ml) of the olive oil, and salt. Mix by hand using a wooden spoon until smooth. Continue working flour, 1/4 cup (28 g) at a time, into the dough until all the flour is incorporated but the dough is still slightly sticky. Turn the dough out onto a lightly floured work surface and knead until smooth but still tacky, 3 to 5 minutes. Coat a large mixing bowl with oil, place the dough into the bowl, and turn to coat all sides. Cover with plastic wrap or clean kitchen towel and place in a warm, draft-free area to double in size, about 1 to 1 1/2 hours. Punch down the dough and divide into two equal portions. Roll each portion into a ball and store in airtight bags or use according to recipe.

[A note about kneading]

To knead dough, start by dusting your hands with flour. Use the heel of your hand to push the dough down and away from you, then turn a 1/2 turn, fold the sides in, and push down and away with the heel of your hand again. Repeat this process to add the flour gradually into the dough.

[Varying flour amounts]

When making pizza dough, the amount of flour needed to complete the dough will vary, depending on the humidity and temperature of your particular location. Always add the last amounts of flour in small (1/4 cup [28 g], for example) increments to avoid overflouring or overworking the dough.

[Freezing dough]

To freeze dough, wrap it in airtight plastic wrap or freezer bags and freeze for up to four months. Before using the dough, thaw in the refrigerator for several hours, or for several hours at room temperature until it begins to rise again and doubles in size. Punch down and use as directed in recipes.

[Makes two 14- to 16-inch (36 – 41 cm) rounds]

No-Oil Neapolitan-Style Pizza **Dough**

The Neapolitan method of making pizza is regarded as true pizza. The *Associazione Verace Pizza Napoletana* (the Association of True Neapolitan Pizza) insists that Neapolitan pizza dough be made using only flour, natural yeast, salt, and water. The dough must be kneaded by hand or using mixers that do not cause the dough to overheat, and it must be punched down and shaped by hand. In keeping with these traditions, this recipe does not employ a food processor.

As mentioned in Chapter 2, Italian flour is different from American all-purpose flour. Italian flour is milled from soft winter wheat, which contains less protein, resulting in a softer crust. To make an authentic Neapolitan dough, I recommend using imported Italian flour or a combination of cake and all-purpose flour. (If using Italian flour, eliminate the all-purpose and cake flours from the recipe.)

1 cup (235 ml) warm water (110°F to 115° F [43°C – 46°C])

1 (¼-ounce [7 g]) package active dry yeast

2 cups (220 g) all-purpose flour

1 cup (110 g) cake flour

1 ½ teaspoon (7.5 g) salt

Olive oil for brushing bowl

Combine the water and yeast in a large mixing bowl, then stir to combine and dissolve yeast. Set aside until foamy, about 5 minutes. Combine the flours in a mixing bowl, and stir using a whisk. In a separate mixing bowl combine 2 cups (220 g) of the flour with the salt, and make a well in the center. Pour the yeast and water mixture into the well, and stir by pulling from the sides with a wooden spoon until the dough comes together. If the dough is too sticky to handle, incorporate an additional ½ cup (55 g) flour. Turn dough out onto a lightly-floured work surface and knead mixture in remaining ½ to 1 cup (55 to 110 g) of flour. Knead the dough until smooth, then shape the dough into a ball.

Coat a large mixing bowl with oil, place the dough into the bowl, and turn to coat all sides. Cover with plastic wrap or clean kitchen towel and place in a warm, draft-free area to double in size. Punch down the dough, divide into two equal portions, and use as directed.

If not using the dough immediately, shape it into two separate balls, coat with oil, place in plastic wrap or airtight bags, and refrigerate overnight before letting the dough rise. When ready to use the dough, bring it to room temperature before letting it rise, then punch it down, divide in half, and proceed with recipe.

The dough can also be frozen after the first kneading. Place in freezer bags or airtight containers, and freeze for up to three months. When ready to use, thaw at room temperature, allow to double in size, then punch down, divide in half, and use according to recipe.

1 (¼ ounce [7 g]) package active dry yeast

1 ¼ cups (295 ml) lukewarm water (110°F to 115°F [43°C – 46°C])

1 ½ cups (165 g) whole wheat flour

½ cup (55 g) flax seed (optional)

1 ½ cups (165 g) [all-purpose flour (2 cups [220 g] if not using flax seed)

1 tablespoon (15 ml) olive oil

1 tablespoon (20 g) honey

½ teaspoon (3 g) kosher salt

[Makes two 14- to 16-inch (36 – 41 cm) rounds]

Whole Wheat and Honey Pizza Dough

Whole wheat pizza dough is as easy to make as basic pizza dough but features a bit more flavor and texture. The optional flax seed adds texture to this dense dough.

Combine the water, yeast, and honey in large mixing bowl, then stir to combine and dissolve the yeast. Set aside until foamy on top, about 5 minutes. Combine the whole wheat and all-purpose flours, flax seed, yeast mixture, oil, and salt in the bowl of a food processor fitted with the blade attachment. Pulse to combine all ingredients. Continue to process until the dough forms a ball. Turn the dough out onto a lightly floured work surface, then knead until smooth and firm. Coat a large mixing bowl with oil, place the dough into the bowl, and turn to coat all sides. Cover with plastic wrap or clean kitchen towel and place in a warm, draft-free area to double in size, about 45 minutes to 1 hour. Punch down the dough, transfer to a lightly floured work surface, and knead briefly. Divide dough into two equal portions, and shape each portion into a ball. If not using dough immediately, place the balls in the refrigerator, then cover, until ready to use. Once ready to use, bring the dough to room temperature. On a lightly floured work surface, roll and stretch the dough into 12- to 16-inch (30 to 41 cm) circles before topping.

1 1/2 cups (355 ml) warm water (110°F to 115°F [43°C – 46°C])

1 teaspoon (4 g) active dry yeast

4 cups (440 g) all-purpose flour

1/2 tablespoon (1 g) dried basil

1/2 tablespoon (1 g) dried marjoram

1/2 tablespoon (1 g) dried thyme

1/2 tablespoon (1 g) dried rosemary

1 tablespoon (18 g) kosher or sea salt

1 teaspoon (5 g) sugar

3 tablespoons (45 ml) olive oil

2 tablespoons (16 g) cornmeal

Combine the water, yeast, and sugar in a large mixing bowl, then stir to combine and dissolve the yeast. Set aside until foamy on top, about 5 minutes. Add in 1 cup (110 g) flour, dried herbs, salt, and 2 tablespoons (30 ml) olive oil until well blended. Mix in 2 1/2 cups (275 g) more flour, 1/2 cup (55 g) at a time, until dough is thick and somewhat sticky.

Turn the dough out onto a lightly-floured work surface and knead the remaining 1/2 cup (55 g) flour into the dough until smooth and elastic. If the dough feels sticky to the touch, knead in additional flour. Coat a large mixing bowl with remaining olive oil, place the dough into the bowl, and turn to coat all sides. Cover with plastic wrap or clean kitchen towel and place in a warm, draft-free area to double in size, about 1 hour. Punch down the dough, divide into two equal portions, shape into balls, wrap with plastic wrap, and refrigerate until ready to use.

[Makes two 14- to 16-inch (36 – 41 cm) rounds]

Herbed Pizza **Dough**

This dough started out as a traditional recipe for *fougasse*, the French version of Italian focaccia bread, but after using it a few times, I realized it also works well for grilled pizza. The amount of flour used will vary depending on location, temperature, and humidity. Add any extra flour 1/2 cup (55 g) at a time to prevent the dough from becoming tough.

1 cup (235 ml) warm water
(110°F to 115°F [43°C – 46°C])

1 (¼-ounce [7 g]) package of
active dry yeast

2 tablespoons (30 g) sugar

1 tablespoon (15 ml) vegetable
oil, plus extra for brushing bowl

2½ cups (275 g) all-purpose flour

½ cup (38 g) semolina flour
or whole wheat flour

3 tablespoons (44 ml)
unsweetened cocoa powder

Combine the water, yeast, and sugar in a large mixing bowl and stir to combine and dissolve the yeast. Set aside until foamy, about 5 minutes. Combine the flour, semolina, and cocoa in a large mixing bowl, then stir with a whisk to combine. To the yeast mixture, add 1½ cups (165 g) of the flour mixture and 1 tablespoon (15 ml) vegetable oil, then mix by hand until fully incorporated and smooth. Continue adding the flour mixture, ¼ cup (28 g) at a time, working the dough after each addition, until all the flour is incorporated. When finished, the dough should still be slightly sticky. Turn the dough out onto a lightly floured work surface and knead until smooth but still slightly sticky, about 3 to 5 minutes. Coat a large mixing bowl with oil, place the dough into the bowl, and turn to coat all sides. Cover with plastic wrap or clean kitchen towel and place in a warm, draft-free area to double in size, about 1 hour. Punch down dough, divide into two portions, and form each portion into a ball. Use immediately as directed or place the dough in airtight plastic bag and refrigerate until ready to use.

If refrigerating before use, remove from refrigerator and bring to room temperature before continuing with recipe. The dough can be kept refrigerated for about 2 days, although you may have to punch it down once or twice during that time. To freeze, place the dough in airtight bags for up to 3 months.

[Makes two 14- to 16-inch (36 – 41 cm) rounds]

Chocolate Pizza **Dough**

Chocolate and pizza, isn't this the ultimate diet? This dough is a superb base for dessert pizzas, either baked or grilled. Grilled strawberries with a drizzle of chocolate are the perfect topping for this sweet indulgence.

1 cup (235 ml) warm water (about 110°F to 115°F [43°C to 46°C])

1 (¼-ounce [7 g]) package active dry yeast

1 tablespoon (20 g) honey

¼ cup (60 g) sugar

3 cups (330 g) all-purpose flour

½ cup (38 g) semolina flour

½ teaspoon (3 g) salt

¼ cup (60 ml) canola oil

Combine the water, yeast, sugar, and honey in small bowl and stir to combine and dissolve yeast. Set aside until a foamy top forms, about 5 minutes. Combine the 2 ½ cups (275 g) flour, semolina, and salt in a large mixing bowl, then make a well in the center. Pour the yeast mixture into the well, then use a wooden spoon to stir the flour vigorously into the well, starting in the center and gradually working out to the sides of the bowl, until the flour is incorporated and the dough begins to hold together. Turn the dough out onto a lightly floured work surface. Knead dough, gradually working in remaining ½ cup (55 g) of flour until the dough is no longer sticky, about 5 minutes.

Continue kneading until the dough is smooth, elastic, and shiny, about 10 minutes. Coat a large mixing bowl with oil, place the dough into the bowl, and turn to coat all sides. Cover with plastic wrap or clean kitchen towel and place in a warm, draft-free area to double in size, about 1½ hours. Punch down the dough. If not using immediately, cover and refrigerate up to 36 hours. If using immediately, turn dough out and prepare according to recipe.

If refrigerating before use, remove from refrigerator and bring to room temperature before continuing with recipe. The dough can be kept refrigerated for about 2 days, although you may have to punch it down once or twice during that time. To freeze, place the dough in airtight bags for up to 3 months.

[Makes two 14- to 16-inch (36 – 41 cm) rounds]

Sweet Pizza **Dough**

Whether as a crust for a dessert pizza or a twist for a savory pie, this dough will boost any flavor. I especially like using this dough with spicy, savory Italian meats and sausages.

4 cups (440 g) all-purpose flour

1 cup (110 g) whole wheat flour

$^1/_2$ cup (38 g) semolina flour

1 tablespoon (5 g) baking powder

$^1/_2$ teaspoon (3 g) kosher salt

1 teaspoon (5 g) sugar

3 tablespoons (42 ml) olive oil

12 ounces (355 ml) dark beer

Combine 3 $^1/_2$ cups (385 g) all-purpose flour, whole wheat flour, semolina, baking powder, salt, and sugar in large mixing bowl, then stir with a whisk to combine thoroughly. Add oil and beer and stir to combine; the resulting dough will be slightly sticky. Place remaining $^1/_2$ cup (55 g) flour on a work surface, turn out dough onto surface, and knead until smooth and firm. If the dough is still too sticky, knead in up to $^1/_2$ cup (55 g) all-purpose flour. Coat a large mixing bowl with oil, place the dough into the bowl, and turn to coat all sides. Cover with plastic wrap or clean kitchen towel and place in a warm, draft-free area to double in size, about 45 minutes to 1 hour. Punch down the dough and shape into two equal portions, then cover and refrigerate if not using right away. If using immediately, divide in half, wrap one portion and refrigerate, then use the other as directed.

[Makes two 14- to 16-inch (36 – 41 cm) rounds]

Dark Beer Crust

This is a hearty, flavorful crust for use in almost any pizza. Developed to complement the German Sausage and Sauerkraut Pizza (see page 93), the flavor of the dough is made intense and robust with the addition of the beer. The natural yeasts and sugars in the beer and the baking soda act as leavening agents, causing it to rise over time.

1 1/2 cups (355 ml) warm water (about 110°F to 115°F [43°C – 46°C])

1 (1/4 ounce [7 g]) package active dry yeast

1 teaspoon (5 g) sugar

3 1/2 cups (385 g) all-purpose flour

1/2 cup (38 g) semolina flour

1/3 cup (75 ml) basil pesto (see recipe, page 20)

1/2 teaspoon (3 g) kosher salt

2 teaspoons (10 ml) olive oil

Combine the water, yeast, and sugar in large mixing bowl, then stir to combine and dissolve the yeast. Set aside until foamy on top, about 5 minutes. To the yeast mixture, add 1 1/2 cups (165 g) flour, semolina, basil pesto, and salt. Mix by hand using a wooden spoon until smooth. Add an additional 1 cup (110 g) flour, working it into the dough thoroughly until incorporated but dough is still sticky. Turn the dough out onto a lightly floured work surface and knead in remaining 1 cup (110 g) of flour. Continue kneading until the dough is smooth but still sticky, about 3 to 5 minutes. Coat a large mixing bowl with oil, place the dough into the bowl, and turn to coat all sides. Cover with plastic wrap or clean kitchen towel and place in a warm, draft-free area to double in size, about 1 to 1 1/2 hours.

Punch down the dough, divide into two equal portions, form into balls, and store in airtight bags or use according to recipe.

[For pizza sticks]
Preheat oven to 400°F (200°C). Stretch dough to a thin rectangular shape measuring about 12" × 9" (31 × 23 cm). Using a pizza cutter, cut 1/2" × 12" (1.5 × 30 cm) strips from the dough. Working with strips, press firmly down on one end and twist the other until the strip is in a spiral formation. Place twists on a nonstick baking sheet, brush with olive oil and sprinkle with sea salt, black pepper, garlic salt, Italian seasoning, or grated Parmesan cheese, or a combination of seasonings. Bake at 400°F (200°C) for 15 minutes, until golden brown. Remove from sheet and let cool on wire rack. Serve warm with tomato sauce, pesto, or herb-infused oils.

[Makes two 14- to 16-inch (36 – 41 cm) rounds]

Basil Pesto Pizza Dough

When used in dough, basil pesto creates a moist, flavorful alternative to the basic pizza dough recipe. You can also use this dough in small twisted strands to make flavorful breadsticks.

Pizza **Dough Alternatives**

If you don't have enough time to make fresh dough, there are plenty of good alternatives available.

[Premade refrigerated dough]
Premade pizza dough is available in most supermarket refrigerated sections.

[Fresh commercial refrigerated dough]
My local supermarket offers three varieties of fresh commercial dough. The supermarket itself packages pizza dough in regular, whole wheat, and foccacia styles.

[Local bakeries]
Many bakeries make their own dough and sell it themselves or to local supermarkets.

[Bread]
Any firm, long-shaped bread works fine for pizza making, including French or Italian bread; you can also use bagels or English muffins. See page 88 for a recipe that uses ciabatta bread.

[Lavash bread]
Lavash is a soft, Armenian bread made in a Tandoor oven that is perfect for thin crust pizzas. See page 96 for a recipe that uses lavash for hors d'oeuvres pizzas. Baking lavash on a pizza stone is the best way to achieve a nice crisp crust.

[Flour tortillas]
Like lavash bread, flour tortillas work well for thin, crispy pizza.

[other basic ingredients]

In addition to dough, some of the recipes in this book call for oven-dried tomatoes, roasted peppers, or roasted garlic. For this reason, I've included those recipes here in the Basics chapter.

[Oven-dried tomatoes]

Makes about 1 cup (50 g)

1 pound (455 g) Roma tomatoes, (about 6 medium-sized tomatoes)

1/4 cup (60 ml) extra-virgin olive oil

1/2 teaspoon (3 g) kosher salt

1/4 teaspoon (0.5 g) coarse ground black pepper

Preheat the oven to 275°F (135°C). Cut tomatoes in half lengthwise. Line a baking sheet with parchment paper and arrange the tomato halves on the tray, cut side facing down. Drizzle each tomato generously with olive oil, then sprinkle with salt and pepper. Bake until the tomatoes begin to shrivel, about 1 hour. When the tomatoes are cool enough to handle, transfer to a container. Pour olive oil over tomatoes to cover, then refrigerate and use as needed.

[Roasted Peppers]

1 pepper yields about 1/2 cup (50 g)

peppers (any color)

olive oil

The easiest way to roast peppers is by using a gas grill. Preheat the grill to high. Coat the peppers evenly with olive oil and place on the grill. Cook the peppers until the skin is charred black, turning them periodically to ensure even roasting. If you do not have a gas grill, I recommend using the broiler in your oven. Preheat the broiler, then place the oiled peppers in a shallow roasting pan under the broiler on the middle rack of the oven. Broil until skin is black, turning them occasionally to ensure even roasting.

Once skin is charred, remove peppers from grill or oven. Place peppers in a brown paper bag and fold the top closed. Let sit for 5 minutes. Remove peppers from bag. The skins should be loosened. Peel away all blackened skin, remove seeds, and slice.

[Roasted garlic]

Roasting concentrates the flavors of raw garlic into an intense, robust, earthy flavor and aroma. Like truffle oil, the flavor and smell of roasted garlic is distinctive and easily recognizable. If you don't like the taste of raw garlic, I encourage you to try this technique, as roasted garlic is unique and enjoyable.

Makes about 1/2 cup (50 g)

4 heads fresh garlic, stem ends removed to 1/2 inch (1.25 cm)

2 tablespoons (30 ml) olive oil

Salt to taste

Coarse ground black pepper

Preheat the oven to 375°F (190°C). Place the garlic, cut ends facing up, in an ovensafe pan or dish. Drizzle each head with olive oil and season with salt and pepper. Cover, then place in oven and roast for 30 to 45 minutes or until garlic is a rich brown, caramelized color and the cloves are easily pierced with the sharp tip of a knife. Remove from oven and let cool. If not using immediately, store refrigerated in an airtight container for up to one week. If using immediately, remove the roasted cloves by pinching the ends of each clove to force the garlic from the skin.

chapter 3

Cooking Tools and Techniqu

Cooking Techniques

[Oven Baking]

For centuries, pizzas were cooked on stone over an open flame. While nothing beats an open flame or a wood-burning stove for a delicious pizza crust, today the modern oven is more practical and well suited for making pizza. All the baking in this book requires an oven temperature of 450°F (230°C). This high heat allows the dough to crisp and bake quickly without burning the ingredients on top. Cheese melts quite fast in such intense heat, so 450°F (230°C) is just right to crisp the dough and melt the cheese at the same time.

If you are serious about pizza—or want a super crisp yet tender crust—you may want to invest in a pizza stone. The pizza stone was designed to emulate the stone bottom of an old-world wood-burning oven. Pizza stones are readily available in houseware departments or kitchen specialty shops and come in a variety of shapes and sizes to fit most any oven. I prefer a large rectangular pizza stone that takes up almost the

entire bottom rack of my oven. This stone lets me bake any size of pizza, from small and round, as well as multiple pies. If you like a crisp bottom crust on your deep-dish pizza, consider a deep-dish stone. You may experience some sticking at first, but the more the stone is used, the more seasoned it becomes, and eventually it will perform almost as well as nonstick Teflon.

As with any new kitchen product, follow the instructions that come with your particular stone regarding proper use and care. With good care, as recommended by the manufacturer, a good stone should last for many years (and many pizzas!).

[Grilling]

Pizza baked in a traditional wood-burning oven has crisp, almost burnt, bottom and edges. Grilling is one of the closest ways to achieve these same traits in pizza. Cooking a thin-crust pizza over an open flame infuses it with a smoked flavor while at the same time producing a beautifully crisp, dark crust.

As with any style of cooking, there are many opinions on how to grill a perfect pizza. I use the following technique: grill the dough, assemble the pizza, then finish it in the oven on a pizza stone. I believe this is the easiest, and oftentimes, fastest, way to get a great grilled pizza on the table.

What type of grill to use is an entirely different subject. A "true" grilled pizza should be made over the open flame of a charcoal- or wood-burning pit. The more common method is to use a gas grill, which will work fine for the recipes in this book.

[Gas grilling]

Because I make grilled pizza quite often and have started giving grilled pizza shells out to friends, I use my gas grill frequently for this method. Most gas grills are not big enough to create the hot and cool zones needed to bake a pizza fully from start to finish, which is why most of the grilled-pizza recipes in this book call for finishing the pizza in the oven on a pizza stone. If you have a gas grill that

offers hot and cool zones, then you can cook your pizza entirely on the grill.

Weber, the brand of my gas grill, makes a wood box that allows you to burn wood chips on a gas grill. This infuses the food with a nice smoked aroma and flavor. I am lucky enough to have a couple of apple trees in my back yard, so in the spring, after pruning, I dry the wood, cut it into sticks, and burn them in my gas grill all summer long.

To prepare for cooking on a gas grill, preheat it to high. Burn off all the excess debris on the grates and brush them down with a steel grill brush. The trick to achieving great grill marks with no sticking is high heat and oil. Oil your dough well before grilling it to eliminate the possibility of sticking. When the grill is fully heated, open the lid and flip the dough, oiled side down, onto the grate. Close the lid, reduce the heat to medium, and grill the dough for about 3 minutes. Open the grill, oil the top of the dough, and flip it over, using a large grilling spatula or tongs.

From this point on, you have only a few minutes to build your pizza and remove the dough from the grill before it burns. I recommend having all your ingredients prepared and nearby if you are going to bake the pizza fully on the

grill. After flipping the dough over, immediately add your toppings, then move the pizza to the cooler zone to finish the baking. Depending on your grill's features, you can also close the lid and turn the heat to low or off to finish baking.

Use a wood or stainless steel pizza peel to transfer your cooked pizza from the grill. Pizza peels are available in a variety of sizes and handle lengths. Before using the peel, be sure to dust it with coarse cornmeal. If you prefer grilling the dough first and finishing in the oven, follow the directions for each recipe in this book accordingly.

[Wood and charcoal grilling]

If you have the luxury of grilling over a wood or charcoal pit, you should keep these basic guidelines in mind: Grilling is a method of cooking directly over high heat, and there are no controls with which to alter the temperature of a wood or charcoal pit other than the location of the heat source. To make it easier, you will need a hot zone and a cool zone on the grill. To achieve this, simply build the fire in one area with a concentration of coals or wood, then gradually spread them out using less wood or coals toward the other side of the grill. The area with the highest concentration of wood or coal will be the hottest.

Here's an easy way to test the heat level of your fire. Hold your hand a few inches above the fire and start counting. If you reach 4 or 5 you have a medium to medium-hot fire; if you can only count to 3 you have a hot fire; and if you quickly remove your hand before getting to 3 you have a very hot fire. For grilling pizza, it is best to build a fire that is hot (a count to 3 or 4) at the high point and medium heat (a 4 to 5 count) on the other side. This allows you to start the pizza over the hot side of the grill, then move it to the medium side for assembling and baking so as not to the char the bottom.

This method of grilling pizza is quite fun and can be very entertaining, but it does take some know-how, practice, and patience. If you have never grilled on an open flame, I recommend starting with a gas grill to get used to the method and then advancing to a charcoal or wood fire.

The most convenient form of charcoal is briquettes, which are made by combining coal and ground wood. Briquettes are easy to light and burn very evenly and efficiently. To build a charcoal fire for grilling, I recommend starting the fire in a chimney starter. This tall, cylindrical-shaped apparatus lets you start the flame in a contained capsule, and then transfer it to the grill. Be sure to follow the manufacturer's instructions. A lot of people use commercial lighter fluid for starting a coal or wood fire, but I believe it gives an undesirable flavor to food, especially dough, which is a sponge for flavor. If you prefer this method, be sure to let the fire burn down a bit before grilling so the fumes from the lighter fluid have time to cook off.

When the coals are red and glowing, move them around the bottom of your grill to create hot and cool zones. For the hot side, pile the lit coals two or three levels deep, then work your way down the grill, reducing the size of the pile to about one level for the cool zone.

To start a hardwood fire, ignite the logs with a combination of kindling and newspaper. Let the logs burn down to hot embers and then arrange them in levels as mentioned above. Cooking with hardwood is one of the best ways to achieve the flavors of wood oven–baked pizza, as the smoke given off by the wood will add flavor to the dough. For a good, hot, long-lasting fire, I recommend oak, hickory, pecan, or fruitwood such as apple.

Appliances

Another option for pizza making at home is the home brick oven. Quite simply, this is a kit that lets you turn your ordinary oven into a brick oven, giving you "surround baking." The kit includes stone sides and a bottom held together with a rack. Quarried tiles or simple bricks are another way of converting your oven into a brick oven. Many grills now come with tiles that are used right on the grill for baking, and these tiles and bricks can be used in the oven just like a stone. Simply place them on the bottom rack of the oven and preheat the oven. If using tiles, be sure that they are quarried, natural, or clay items that are not glazed or treated in any way.

Another of my favorite cooking appliances is a cast iron skillet. I have several cast iron skillets of varying sizes that are great for cooking. Several recipes in this book, such as the Buffalo Chicken Skillet Pizza, call for a cast iron pan. Cast iron, like a pizza stone, becomes more seasoned over time. With proper care and seasoning, a cast iron pan can last a lifetime (or more). My favorite recent discovery is the cast-iron pizza pan made by Lodge. I love this pan, and it spoils all cooks who are new to cast iron because it comes pre-seasoned. I don't encourage cooking a pizza in any oven-proof skillet, but cast iron will hold up fine in the oven.

chapter 4

Classic Pizza

What determines a classic pizza? I define it by the ingredients used to make the pizza and its place in history. Pepperoni pizza, for example, is a classic; it has been around for years and is, by far, one of—if not the most—commonly ordered pizzas today. Black olive and pesto pizza is another classic, both because of its place in pizza history and because New York pizzerias have served it for decades. Probably the most recognized classic is Pizza Margherita, which has been around for more than 100 years.

The pizza recipes in this chapter have either stood the test of time or are adaptations of classical ingredients and techniques. Whether they originate with the old-world bakers of Naples or the modern chefs in New York and Chicago pizzerias, these pizzas are classics for a reason—they all taste delicious.

1 round Basic Pizza Dough (see page 22)

1 (28-ounce [795 g]) can peeled plum tomatoes, drained and seeded

3 tablespoons (45 ml) extra virgin olive oil

2 cloves garlic, finely chopped

1/2 teaspoon (3 g) salt

1 tablespoon (8 g) coarse cornmeal

6 ounces (170 g) fresh mozzarella cheese, thinly sliced

8 fresh basil leaves, torn

1/4 cup (7 g) fresh shredded Parmesan cheese

Preheat oven to 450°F (230°C) with pizza stone (if using). Cut tomatoes in chunks and place in a mixing bowl with 2 tablespoons olive oil, garlic, and salt. Stretch pizza dough to a round disc to fit your pizza pan or stone. Dust peel or pan with cornmeal, place stretched dough on peel, top with tomatoes and cheese, and drizzle with remaining olive oil. Transfer dough to pizza stone or pan and bake for 8 to 10 minutes or until dough is golden brown and cheese is bubbling. Remove from oven using peel and sprinkle with Parmesan cheese and basil. Slice and serve.

[Serves 4]

Pizza **Margherita**

This classic pizza combines tomato sauce, fresh mozzarella cheese, and fresh basil leaves as a tribute to the national colors of Italy.

[Serves 4]

Spinach-Stuffed Pizza

Anyone who hails from Chicago will like this thick, hearty, spinach-stuffed pizza. This pie has a nice chewy crust and layers of delicious flavors. If you want a vegetarian version, just omit the Canadian bacon and add more mushrooms.

1 round Basic Pizza Dough
(see page 22)

1 tablespoon (15 ml) olive oil

2 (10-ounce [280 g]) bags
baby spinach, washed

3 ounces (85 g) Canadian
bacon, diced

1 teaspoon (1 g) dried oregano

2 cloves garlic, sliced thin

2 ounces (55 g)
mushrooms, sliced

8 ounces (225 g)
shredded mozzarella cheese

½ cup (120 ml) Basic Tomato
Sauce (see recipe, page 17),
or Spicy Tomato Sauce (see
recipe, page 19)

2 tablespoons (10 g)
grated Parmesan cheese

Preheat oven to 450°F (230°C) with pizza stone (if using). In a large skillet, heat olive oil over medium-high heat, then add spinach and wilt for 2 minutes. Remove from heat and transfer to a mixing bowl. Add Canadian bacon, oregano, garlic, and mushrooms to the wilted spinach and stir to combine thoroughly. Roll out dough to about 18 inches (46 cm). To make bottom crust, spread dough in bottom of greased 14-inch (36-cm)-deep-dish pizza pan and up the sides. Spread mozzarella evenly over bottom crust, then add spinach mixture and cover with top crust. Seal the two dough edges together using your fingers, and trim any excess. Slit the top crust to allow steam to vent during baking. Cover top crust evenly with tomato sauce, then sprinkle with Parmesan cheese. Transfer to lower rack of oven or directly onto pizza stone, and bake for 45 minutes or until crust is golden brown. Remove from pan and cool 5 minutes on a wire rack. Cut and serve.

[Serves 4]

BBQ Chicken Pizza with Smoked Gouda and Grilled Pineapples

Smoked Gouda is truly a great cheese for pizza. If you've never grilled pineapple, you should really try it; the flavors are fresh and intense.

1 round Basic Pizza Dough (see page 22)

Olive oil for brushing dough

2 (8-ounce [225 g]) boneless, skinless chicken breasts

1 cup (235 ml) favorite barbecue sauce, divided

1 teaspoon (2 g) coarse ground black pepper

1 golden pineapple, peeled and cut into $^1/_2$-inch (1.3 cm)-thick slices

2 tablespoons (30 ml) vegetable oil

4 ounces (115 g) shredded mozzarella cheese

6 ounces (170 g) shredded smoked Gouda cheese

4 ounces (115 g) Canadian bacon, chopped

$^1/_4$ cup (15 g) loosely packed cilantro leaves

1 tablespoon (8 g) coarse cornmeal

Preheat grill to high. Toss the chicken breast with $^1/_2$ cup (120 ml) of the barbecue sauce and the black pepper in a large mixing bowl. Cover and refrigerate for at least 30 minutes. Stretch dough to a 16-inch (41-cm) round. Oil and grill one side at a time until golden and crisp, about 3 minutes per side. Dust peel or pan with cornmeal. Transfer to pizza crust to pan or peel. Preheat oven to 450°F (230°C) with pizza stone (if using). Coat pineapple slices with vegetable oil, place on hot grill, and cook until browned on each side, about 5 minutes per side. Transfer to dish and let cool. When cool enough to handle, remove core section of each slice and chop into large chunks. Grill chicken until cooked through, about 7 minutes per side. Transfer to plate and let cool. When cool enough to handle, cut or shred into strips. Top grilled dough with mozzarella cheese and half of Gouda. Add chopped pineapple, chicken, and Canadian bacon, then sprinkle with remaining Gouda. Transfer to pizza stone and cook until cheese is bubbling, about 5 minutes. Remove from oven and let sit for 5 minutes, then top with cilantro. Slice and serve.

Meatball and Tomato Stew Grilled Pizza

Save any leftover meatballs from this recipe for use on pasta or in a meatball sandwich.

FOR THE SAUCE:

1 (28-ounce [795 g]) can diced tomatoes

1 (28-ounce [795 g]) can tomato sauce

1/2 cup (15 g) packed fresh basil leaves, roughly chopped

6 ounces (170 g) baby bella mushrooms, stems removed and reserved, caps chopped

6 cloves garlic, sliced thin

1 (6-ounce [170 g]) can small ripe olives, chopped

3 tablespoons (45 ml) red wine vinegar

1/4 teaspoon (1.5 g) kosher salt

1/2 teaspoon (0.5 g) coarse ground black pepper

1/4 teaspoon (0.3 g) crushed red pepper flakes

FOR THE MEATBALLS:

2 tablespoons (30 ml) olive oil

1/3 cup (40 g) finely chopped red onion

1 tablespoon (10 g) chopped garlic

Reserved stems from baby bella mushrooms, chopped fine

1 pound (455 g) ground sirloin

1/2 pound (225 g) ground sweet Italian sausage, casing removed

2 large eggs

1 tablespoon (4 g) chopped fresh Italian flat-leaf parsley

3 tablespoons (15 g) freshly grated Parmesan cheese

1/4 cup (28 g) seasoned bread crumbs

1/2 teaspoon (0.6 g) dried oregano

1/2 teaspoon (3 g) kosher salt

1/4 teaspoon (0.5 g) coarse ground black pepper

1/8 teaspoon (0.3 g) ground nutmeg

2 tablespoons (30 ml) vegetable oil for frying

FOR THE PIZZA:

1 round Basic Pizza Dough (see page 22)

2 cups (225 g) shredded mozzarella cheese

2 tablespoons (10 g) grated Parmesan cheese

1/4 cup (20 g) shredded Asiago cheese

1/3 cup (80 g) ricotta cheese

1 egg

1 tablespoon (8 g) coarse cornmeal

2 tablespoons (5 g) fresh basil, chopped

1/4 teaspoon (1.5 g) kosher salt

1/4 teaspoon (1.5 g) coarse ground black pepper

meatballs, turning to cook on all sides. Once browned on all sides, transfer meatballs directly to sauce; do not drain or let cool. Repeat to cook remaining meatballs, adding vegetable oil as needed. Mix meatballs to cover with sauce and cook for 45 minutes to 1 hour longer.

[For the Pizza]
Preheat oven to 450°F (230°C) with pizza stone (if using). Dust peel or pan with cornmeal. Stretch the dough into a large circle and place on pizza pan or peel. Combine the ricotta, egg, basil, salt, and pepper in a small mixing bowl and stir to incorporate egg thoroughly. Top dough with 1 cup (235 ml) tomato sauce in an even layer, then sprinkle with Parmesan, Asiago, and mozzarella cheese. Remove meatballs from sauce and slice. Add sliced meatballs to pizza, then top randomly with spoonfuls of ricotta cheese mixture. Transfer to pizza stone or oven and bake until golden and cheese is bubbling, about 15 minutes. Remove form oven and let rest for 5 minutes. Slice and serve.

[For the Sauce and Meatballs]
Combine all the ingredients for the sauce in a large stock pot and bring to a boil. Reduce heat and simmer for 1 hour.

Meanwhile, prepare the meatballs. Heat the olive oil in a large skillet over medium-high heat. Add the onion, garlic, and mushroom stems and sauté until tender, about 5 minutes. Remove and let cool.

Combine the sirloin, sausage, eggs, parsley, Parmesan cheese, bread crumbs, nutmeg, oregano, salt, pepper, and cooled mushroom mixture in a large mixing bowl. Use your hands to combine all the ingredients thoroughly, then form into 2" (5 cm) round balls and set aside.

Heat the vegetable oil in a large skillet over medium heat, then sauté first batch of

1 round Basic Pizza Dough
(see page 22)

2 (8-ounce [225 g])
boneless, skinless chicken
breasts

Asian ginger habachi
grilling sauce

2 tablespoons (28 g) butter

2 tablespoons (30 ml) olive oil

4 ounces (115 g)
shitake mushrooms, thinly sliced

1 medium red onion, sliced

3 cloves roasted garlic
(see technique, page 33)

1 cup (235 ml) Basil Pesto
(see recipe, page 20)

4 ounces (115 g) shredded
Asiago cheese

6 ounces (170 g)
shredded mozzarella cheese

1 cup (50 g) shredded radicchio

8 leaves fresh basil, torn

1 tablespoon (8 g)
coarse cornmeal

Preheat grill to high. Preheat oven to 450°F (230°C) with pizza stone (if using).

Toss chicken breast with habachi grilling sauce in a mixing bowl. Cover and refrigerate for at least 30 minutes. Melt the butter with the olive oil over high heat in a large skillet, then sauté the onions for 3 minutes. Add the mushrooms and roasted garlic and continue to sauté until the mushrooms and onions are tender, 3 minutes more. Transfer to bowl and set aside. Stretch dough to a large rectangular shape. Oil and grill one side at a time until golden and crisp, about 3 minutes per side. Dust pan or peel with cornmeal. Transfer grilled dough to a pizza stone or pan. Grill chicken until cooked through, about 7 minutes on each side. Remove and let cool. When cool enough to handle, slice into thin strips. Top grilled dough with basil pesto followed by Asiago and mozzarella cheese, mushroom mixture, and sliced chicken. Bake on stone or pan until cheese is melted and bubbling, about 10 minutes. Remove and top with radicchio and basil. Slice and serve.

[Serves 4]

Wood-Grilled Chicken Pizza with Radicchio and Feta

If you have the ability to grill over wood, it is worth the time and effort. Most gas grills offer accessories for hardwood grilling, and the results are almost as good.

1 round Basic Pizza Dough
(see page 22)

2 tablespoons (28 ml) olive
oil, plus extra for brushing dough

3 tablespoons (45 g) butter

4 leeks, cleaned, white
parts sliced thin

4 tablespoons (60 g) sugar

1/4 cup (60 ml) heavy cream

Salt

Black pepper

3 tablespoons (15 g)
grated Parmesan cheese

8 ounces (225 g) shredded
Gruyere cheese

2 pounds (1 kg) Yukon
gold potatoes, sliced thin

1/4 cup (25 g) sliced
scallions, green and white parts

Preheat grill to high. Preheat oven to 450°F (230°C) with pizza stone (if using). Stretch dough into a large rectangle. Oil and grill one side at a time until golden and crisp, about 3 minutes per side. Transfer to a pizza pan or peel. Heat olive oil and butter in a large skillet over medium-high heat, then add leeks and sauté on high for 3 minutes until just tender. Reduce heat to medium, add sugar, stir to combine and cook, stirring occasionally, for about 10 minutes, to caramelize leeks. Don't let leeks burn or get crisp. Once browned, add heavy cream and reduce to a thick consistency, about 2 minutes. Remove from heat and set aside. Sprinkle grilled dough with an even layer of Parmesan followed by Gruyere, then top with an even layer of potatoes followed by leeks. Transfer to oven and bake until golden and bubbling, about 15 minutes. Remove, sprinkle with scallions, and let sit for 5 minutes. Slice and serve.

[Serves 4]

Caramelized Leek and Golden Potato Grilled Pizza

Golden potatoes are a tender and flavorful addition to any pizza. The raw slices take a little longer to cook, so the ingredients that accompany them must be able to hold up to longer times in the oven. Slice the potatoes as thinly as possible by hand or using a mandolin.

1 round Basic Pizza Dough
(see page 22)
or Herbed Pizza Dough
(see page 26)

Olive oil for brushing

¼ cup (20 g) grated
Pecorino Romano cheese

6 ounces (170 g)
shredded mozzarella cheese

4 ounces (115 g) shredded
Asiago cheese

½ cup (30 g) chopped
mixed fresh herbs, such as
rosemary, flat-leaf parsley,
chives, and basil

4 ounces (115 g) shredded
creamy Havarti cheese

½ cup (60 g) crumbled
feta cheese

1 tablespoon (8 g)
coarse cornmeal

Preheat grill to high. Preheat oven to 450°F (230°C) with pizza stone (if using). Dust peel or pan with cornmeal. Stretch or roll dough into a large roughly rectangular shape. Oil and grill one side at a time until golden and crisp, about 3 minutes per side. Transfer dough to a pizza pan or peel. Brush grilled dough with olive oil, then sprinkle evenly with Pecorino cheese. Toss together mozzarella, fresh herbs, and Asiago cheese in a small mixing bowl. Spread mixture evenly over the top of grilled dough then top with Pecorino and Havarti and sprinkle with feta. Transfer to pizza stone or bottom rack of oven and bake until cheese is bubbling and golden. Remove and let rest 5 minutes. Slice and serve.

[Variations to the recipe]
This recipe is great as is, but for a little spice, try one of the dough variations listed on page 32. Explore the cheese aisle of your local grocer and substitute some interesting cheeses to alter the flavors. Instead of feta, for instance, try crumbled goat cheese or Gorgonzola. Or try topping the entire pizza with shaved Parmigiano-Reggiano or a specialty oil. To turn this flavorful pizza into a gourmet experience, add shaved black truffle and a sprinkle of white truffle oil after baking; the flavors are very intense and enjoyable.

[Serves 4]

Cheesiest Cheesy and Herb Pizza

This recipe celebrates cheese, combined with fresh herbs, for an intensely flavorful pie. Any number of fresh herbs will work with this recipe, so feel free to experiment.

1 round Basic Pizza Dough
(see page 22)

12 ounces (340 g) assorted
wild mushrooms, such as shitake,
oyster, and baby bella

3 tablespoons (30 g)
chopped fresh garlic

1 teaspoon (2 g) coarse
ground black pepper

$^1\!/_2$ teaspoon (3 g) kosher salt

3 tablespoons (45 ml) olive
oil, plus extra for grilling dough

2 tablespoons (28 g) butter

$^1\!/_2$ cup (40 g) grated
Romano cheese

8 ounces (225 g)
Shredded mozzarella cheese

4 ounces (115 g)
pancetta, chopped

$^1\!/_4$ cup (40 g) crumbled
feta cheese

Roasted Wild Mushroom Pizza with Pancetta and Feta

This pizza combines the concentrated flavors of roasted mushrooms and garlic for an earthy, intense taste. Adding pancetta (Italian bacon), with its salty taste, to the mix brings this over the top. For a vegetarian version, just leave off the pancetta.

Preheat oven to 350°F (180°C) with pizza stone (if using). Remove the stems and slice mushrooms thin, then transfer to a roasting pan and toss with garlic, black pepper, salt, and olive oil. Dot the mushrooms with butter and roast, stirring occasionally, until tender and browned, about 30 minutes. Remove from oven and let cool.

Pan fry the pancetta in a small skillet over medium-high heat until browned, about 7 minutes. Transfer to bowl and let cool. Stretch dough into thin circle. Preheat grill to high. Oil and grill one side of dough until browned and crisp, about 3 minutes.

Turn dough over, reduce grill heat to low, and top with even layers of Romano, mozzarella, and mushroom mixture.

Sprinkle with pancetta and feta cheese. Close grill lid and cook until cheeses are melted. Remove from grill and let sit for 5 minutes. Slice and serve.

1 round Basic Pizza Dough
(see page 22)

3 (6-ounce [170 g])
boneless, skinless chicken
breasts, trimmed and cut in half

3 tablespoons (30 g)
chopped fresh garlic

3 tablespoons (45 ml)
olive oil, plus extra for
grilling dough

2 teaspoons (4 g) coarse
ground black pepper

2 tablespoons (10 g)
grated Romano cheese

6 ounces (170 g) shredded
white cheddar cheese

3 ounces (85 g) sliced pepperoni

2 ounces (55 g) baby
spinach leaves

6 ounces (170 g) shredded
smoked Gouda cheese

[Serves 4]

Garlic-Grilled Chicken and Pepperoni Pizza with Smoked Gouda

It is possible that this spectacular pizza, which uses smoked Gouda cheese, will become your favorite pizza.

Preheat grill to high. Preheat oven to 450°F (230°C) with pizza stone (if using). Toss chicken with garlic, olive oil, and black pepper in a mixing bowl. Cover and refrigerate for at least 30 minutes. Stretch dough into a thin, rough circle. Oil and grill one side at a time until golden and crisp, about 3 minutes per side. Dust peel or pan with cornmeal. Place grilled dough on peel.

Grill chicken for 7 minutes on each side until browned and tender. Remove from grill and let cool. When cool enough to handle, slice into thin strips.

Top grilled dough with even layers of Romano, Cheddar, pepperoni, spinach, and Gouda. Add shredded chicken, transfer to stone, and bake until cheese is melted and starting to brown, about 15 minutes. Remove and let sit for 5 minutes. Slice and serve.

New York–Style Stone-Baked Pizza

Short of having a wood-burning oven in your home, this is a great way to make an authentic "New York" pizza.

1 round Basic Pizza Dough (see page 22)

Extra-virgin olive oil

8 ounces (225 g) shredded mozzarella cheese

8 ounces (225 g) ground sweet Italian sausage, cooked and crumbled

12 ounces (340 g) meatballs, sliced (see recipe, page 42)

3 cloves fresh garlic, chopped

1 ½ cups (355 ml) Basic Tomato Sauce (see recipe, page 17)

¼ cup (15 g) loosely packed fresh basil leaves, roughly torn

1 tablespoon (8 g) coarse cornmeal

Preheat grill to high with pizza stone (if using). Stretch dough to a thin round. Oil and grill one side at a time until golden and crisp, about 3 minutes per side. Dust peel or pan with cornmeal. Place grilled dough on pizza peel. Drizzle dough with olive oil, then spread an even layer of tomato sauce, reserving ½ cup (115 ml). Top with mozzarella, sprinkle with garlic, add crumbled sausage and sliced meatballs, then dot with remaining ½ cup (115 ml) tomato sauce. Transfer pizza to stone and bake for 15 minutes, or until cheese is melted and starting to brown. Remove, sprinkle with fresh basil, and let sit for 5 minutes. Slice and serve.

1 round Basic Pizza Dough
(see page 22)

½ pound (225 g)
thick asparagus spears

Extra-virgin olive oil

Coarse ground black pepper

2 tablespoons (10 g)
freshly grated Romano cheese

8 ounces (225 g)
shredded mozzarella cheese

3 ounces (85 g) crumbled
goat cheese

1 teaspoon (1.25 g) chopped
fresh tarragon

1 teaspoon (1.25 g) chopped
fresh Italian flat-leaf parsley

White truffle oil

1 ounce (28 g) shaved fresh
Parmigiano-Reggiano cheese

Grilled Asparagus and Cheese Pizza with White Truffle Oil

Asparagus and truffle oil, in my mind, are designed to be together. If you have never had the pleasure of tasting truffle oil, treat yourself this time— the taste is distinctive and addictive. Although truffle oil is expensive, I feel it is worth the investment. Only a little drizzle is needed for most cooking applications, as it is pungent in flavor and aroma. It is available in gourmet food stores and the oil aisle of most supermarkets.

Preheat grill to high. Preheat oven to 450°F (230°C) with pizza stone (if using). Remove bands from asparagus. Holding one spear in both hands, snap the spear in half; the spear should break where the tough end meets the tender top. Place snapped spears on cutting board and line up tops, then trim all spears to the same length. Place spears on a platter, drizzle with olive oil, and sprinkle generously with black pepper. Grill spears until tender, turning periodically, about 10 minutes. Remove and let cool. When cool enough to handle, slice in half lengthwise and set aside. Stretch dough into a thin rectangle. Oil and grill one side at a time until golden and crisp, about 3 minutes per side. Transfer to pizza stone or baking sheet.

Top grilled dough with Romano, mozzarella, and sliced asparagus spears. Top with goat cheese and sprinkle with tarragon and parsley. Place on middle rack of hot oven and bake until cheese is melted and starting to brown, about 15 minutes. Remove and let sit for 5 minutes. Drizzle with truffle oil, then slice and serve.

Individual Grilled Greek-Style Pizza

These personal-size pizzas are perfect for any pizza party. Any topping combination is great for this application, just divide the dough into smaller rounds and prepare as directed.

1 recipe Basic Pizza Dough (see page 22)

4 tablespoons (60 ml) olive oil, plus additional for coating pizza dough

1 pound (455 g) beef flank steak or skirt steak

Coarse ground black pepper, for steak rub

1 pint (300 g) grape tomatoes

1 cup (100 g) Kalamata olives, pitted and chopped

1 tablespoon (4 g) dried oregano

1 eggplant, peeled and sliced into ½-inch (1 cm)-thick slices

8 ounces (225 g) shredded Monterey jack cheese

8 ounces (225 g) feta cheese, cut into chunks (or crumbled)

1 tablespoon (4 g) fresh cilantro, chopped

Cilantro Mint Pesto (recipe follows)

CILANTRO MINT PESTO:
Makes about 1 cup (300 g)

1 cup (50 g) fresh cilantro, chopped

¼ cup (15 g) fresh mint, chopped

3 cloves fresh garlic, peeled

2 tablespoons (30 ml) freshly squeezed lemon juice

¼ teaspoon (0.5 g) coarse ground black pepper

Pinch of salt

1 cup (225 g) extra-virgin olive oil

1 tablespoon (15 ml) plain yogurt

¼ cup (25 g) grated parmesan cheese

2 tablespoons (10 g) grated Asiago cheese

[To make the Cilantro Mint Pesto]

In the bowl of a food processor fitted with the blade attachment, add the cilantro, mint, garlic, lemon juice, salt, and black pepper. Pulse to chop the ingredients. With the processor running, add the olive oil in a steady stream. Blend until a thick puree is achieved. Remove from processor and place in a small mixing bowl. Add the yogurt, Parmesan, and Asiago cheese and combine. Set aside until needed. Can be jarred and refrigerated for up to one week.

Preheat oven to 375°F (190°C). Preheat outdoor grill to high heat. Place beef on a plate, rub aggressively and evenly with coarse ground black pepper, and then grill until cooked through as desired. When cool enough to handle, slice beef. In a medium-sized mixing bowl, combine tomatoes, Kalamata olives, and oregano. Toss with 2 tablespoons olive oil. Place on a baking sheet in a single even layer, and roast in oven for about 15 minutes; tomatoes should begin to blister and pop.

Place eggplant slices on a plate and brush with 2 tablespoons olive oil, coating evenly. Place on hot grill and cook about 5 minutes per side, or until tender and browned. Remove from heat; cool until able to handle. Cut into cubes and set aside. Make sure to clean your grill grates after cooking eggplant slices.

Divide pizza dough into 4 individual rounds. Use your hands to stretch the dough into a thin rectangular shape. Use rolling pin if necessary to achieve a thin dough. Brush one side of each round evenly with olive oil. Place each pizza round on hot grill, oil side down. Grill dough for 3 minutes. While rounds are grilling, oil remaining sides. Flip dough over and reduce heat to low.

Top each with ingredients, beginning with an even coating of Cilantro Mint Pesto. Sprinkle with Monterey jack cheese, then tomatoes and kalamata olives, followed by sliced beef, feta cheese chunks, and chopped cilantro. Close grill lid and let cook until cheese is melted. If the bottom of dough begins to get too browned, turn off heat and leave lid closed until cheese is melted. Using a wooden or aluminum pizza peel, remove the pizzas and place on a cutting board. Let sit for 5 minutes before cutting. Cut and serve.

1 round Whole Wheat and Honey Pizza Dough (see page 25)

1 cup (235 ml) Basil Pesto (see page 20)

8 ounces (225 g) fresh mozzarella cheese, sliced

1 (4-ounce [115 g]) can sliced black olives

2 tablespoons (10 g) grated Parmesan cheese

1 tablespoon (8 g) coarse cornmeal

Preheat oven to 450°F (230°C) with pizza stone (if using). Stretch dough into a 16-inch (41-cm) inch round. Dust pan or peel with cornmeal and top with dough. Top dough with an even layer of pesto, followed by mozzarella and olives, then sprinkle with Parmesan cheese. Transfer to pizza stone and bake until golden and bubbling, about 20 minutes. Remove and let sit for 5 minutes. Slice and serve.

[Serves 4]

Pesto and Black Olive Pizza

Just about every pizzeria in New York City serves a version of this classic combination. The traditional recipe calls for sliced black olives, but feel free to experiment with your favorites.

1 recipe Basic Pizza Dough
(see page 22)

3 tablespoons (45 ml) olive
oil, plus extra for greasing pan

¼ pound (115 g) ground
sweet Italian sausage

3 medium green peppers, sliced
into thin strips

2 medium white onions, cut in
half and thinly sliced

4 cloves garlic, minced

6 ounces (170 g) provolone
cheese, thinly sliced

8 ounces (225 g)
shredded mozzarella cheese

½ cup (120 ml) Basic Tomato Sauce
(see recipe, page 17)

¼ cup (25 g) grated
Parmesan cheese

Coarse cornmeal (if using
deep-dish pizza stone)

[Serves 6]

Chicago-Style Deep Dish Pizza

Traditional Chicago-style pizza is deep-dish with a thick, tender crust. This classic recipe combines tender peppers and onions with a thick layer of cheese and tomato sauce.

Preheat oven to 450°F (230°C). Heat 1 tablespoon (15 ml) olive oil over medium-high heat in a large skillet, then add the ground sausage and cook until browned. Transfer sausage to bowl, leaving behind pan drippings, then add remaining olive oil and heat. Sauté peppers, onions, and garlic until tender, about 4 minutes. (Take care not to overcook.) Remove from heat and set aside.

Divide dough in half, then roll out one portion to 2 inches (5 cm) wider than deep-dish pizza pan. If using a metal pan, grease the bottom and sides; if using a deep-dish pizza stone, coat the bottom with coarse cornmeal. Place dough in the bottom and up the sides of the pan. Bake the dough for about 4 minutes, until it just begins to crisp. Remove from oven and layer bottom with provolone cheese followed by mozzarella, peppers, onions, and sausage.

Roll out second dough portion to same size as first round and place over cheese, peppers, onions, and sausage. Seal the two edges together with your fingers; be sure to create a well in the dough to allow for tomato sauce, then trim away any excess. Slit the top crust to allow steam to vent during baking. Add tomato sauce in an even layer over dough and sprinkle with Parmesan cheese.

Bake on lower rack of oven for about 45 minutes or until crust is golden brown and sauce is bubbling. Remove from pan and let sit for 5 minutes. Cut and serve.

1 round Herbed Pizza Dough
(see page 26)

1 cup (250 g) ricotta cheese

2 heads roasted garlic
(see page 33), garlic squeezed
from each clove

1 tablespoon (4 g) dried oregano

Salt

Black pepper

2 tablespoons (30 ml) olive oil

8 ounces (225 g)
sliced provolone cheese

6 ounces (170 g)
shredded mozzarella cheese

½ bunch broccoli rabe,
blanched, dried, and chopped

2 ounces (55 g) shaved
Parmigiano-Reggiano cheese

[Serves 4]

Pizza **Bianca with Roasted Garlic, Ricotta, and Broccoli Rabe**

Pizzas without tomatoes or tomato sauce in Italy are called *bianca*, which means white. This white pizza combines broccoli rabe, roasted garlic, ricotta, and Parmigiano-Reggiano for a flavorful result.

Preheat oven to 450°F (230°C) with pizza stone (if using). Combine ricotta, roasted garlic, and oregano in a mixing bowl and season with salt and pepper. Stretch the dough into a 16-inch (41-cm) round. Dust pizza peel with cornmeal and place dough on peel. Brush dough evenly with olive oil, then top with provolone and mozzarella, followed by broccoli rabe. Spoon ricotta mixture over rabe. Transfer to pizza stone or pan and bake until golden and bubbling, about 15 minutes. Remove and let sit for 5 minutes. Top with shaved Parmigiano-Reggiano cheese. Slice and serve.

Pizza

2 recipes Basic Pizza Dough (see page 22)

2 cups (475 ml) Spicy Tomato Sauce (see page 18), divided

¼ cup (20 g) grated Romano cheese

6 ounces (170 g) sliced provolone cheese

½ pound (225 g) hard salami, thinly sliced

½ pound (225 g) hot capicola, thinly sliced

12 leaves fresh basil

¼ pound (115 g) pepperoni, thinly sliced

¼ pound (150 g) prosciutto, thinly sliced

Olive oil for brushing dough

1 tablespoon (8 g) coarse cornmeal

Preheat oven to 450°F (230°C) with pizza stone (if using). Reserve 1 cup (235 ml) sauce for dipping. Divide dough evenly into six individual balls. Stretch each ball of dough into an 8-inch (20 cm) round. Divide ingredients evenly among rounds: sprinkle with Romano cheese, then layer one half of each round with tomato sauce, followed by provolone cheese, hard salami, capicola, basil, pepperoni, and prosciutto; finish with provolone cheese. Fold and stretch dough over filling to form a half circle; seal by pinching dough together between thumb and fingers while rolling up and over at the same time. Work around entire perimeter of the calzone. Repeat process with 5 remaining dough rounds. Dust peel or pan with cornmeal. Place calzones on peel; brush tops, sides, and pinched edges with olive oil, then cut three small (½ inch [1.3 cm]) slits in the top of each calzone to release steam during baking. Bake until golden brown, about 15 minutes. Remove from oven and let sit 5 minutes. Warm reserved tomato sauce and serve.

[Serves 6]

Deli Counter Calzone

Calzones can be stuffed with just about anything. For variation, visit your favorite deli counter and ask for a variety of Italian deli meats.

1 round Basic Pizza Dough (see page 22)

½ pound (225 g) ziti, cooked and drained

3 tablespoons (45 ml) olive oil

4 ounces (115 g) pancetta, sliced thick and diced

2 tablespoons (20 g) chopped fresh garlic

2 (8-ounce [225 g]) boneless, skinless chicken breasts, diced

1 cup (235 ml) white wine

Juice of one lemon

Juice of one orange

4 tablespoons (55 g) cold butter, cut into chunks

Salt

Coarse ground black pepper

6 ounces (170 g) shredded mozzarella cheese

8 ounces (225 g) fresh marinated mozzarella balls

10 leaves fresh basil

3 ounces (85 g) shaved Parmigiano-Reggiano cheese

1 tablespoon (8 g) coarse cornmeal

[Serves 4]

Ziti Pizza with Citrus Chicken and Mozzarella

Chicken over pasta is a staple in my house, and this recipe brings that combination to a grilled pizza.

Cook ziti in boiling salted water according to package instructions. Drain and rinse under cold water, then set aside. Preheat grill to high. Preheat oven to 450°F (230°C) with pizza stone (if using). Heat 1 tablespoon (15 ml) olive oil in a large skillet over medium-high heat. Add pancetta and cook until crisp and browned. Transfer to paper towel, then set pancetta aside. Reserve rendered fat.

Add remaining olive oil (adjusting amount to equal 2 tablespoons with the addition of fat rendered from pancetta. Add chicken and cook until brown, about 10 minutes. Halfway through cooking the chicken, add the garlic. When cooked through, remove chicken and set aside. Deglaze pan with white wine, scraping bottom of pan to release drippings, and reduce by half. Add lemon and orange juices, then gradually whisk in cold butter, a few chunks at a time, to create a thick sauce. Season with salt and pepper. Stretch dough into a large round, then oil and grill one side at a time until browned and crisp, about 3 minutes.

Dust peel or pan with corn meal. Transfer grilled dough to pizza peel, top with mozzarella, and transfer to stone and bake until cheese is melted and bubbling, about 10 minutes. Toss ziti with chicken, mozzarella balls, basil, and hot citrus sauce in large bowl. Remove pizza from oven and top immediately with pasta mixture, then finish with Parmigiano-Reggiano. Slice and serve.

1 round Basic Pizza Dough
(see page 22)

2 heads roasted garlic
(see page 33)

4 tablespoons (55 g) butter

2 tablespoons (30 ml) olive oil

1 pound (455 g) fresh
clams, chopped

2 tablespoons (8 g) fresh
chopped Italian flat-leaf parsley

2 tablespoons (10 g)
grated Parmesan cheese

1/2 cup (120 ml) dry white wine

8 ounces (225 g)
shredded mozzarella cheese

4 ounces (115 g) shredded
fontina cheese

Preheat oven to 450°F (230°C) with pizza stone (if using). Melt butter with 1 tablespoon (15 ml) olive oil in a large skillet over medium-high heat. Add clams and sauté for 1 minute, then add roasted garlic and stir to combine, about 3 minutes. Remove from heat and toss in parsley, then season with salt and pepper.

Stretch dough into very thin rough circle. Dust peel with cornmeal. Place dough on pizza peel, then spoon some of the clam sauce (without the clams) onto the dough and brush to coat the entire dough. Top with even layers of Parmesan, mozzarella, and fontina cheeses. Top with remaining clam mixture, then transfer to pizza stone or pan and bake until golden and cheese is bubbling, about 15 minutes. Remove and let sit for 5 minutes. Slice and serve.

[Serves 4]

Clam and Roasted Garlic Thin-Crust Pizza

Some people aren't too fond of clams or scallops on their pizza, but this recipe is worth a try—the flavors are simple and great.

chapter 5

Contemporary Pizza

It wasn't long ago that pizza ingredients never varied much from tomato sauce, Italian sausage, pepperoni, and a limited selection of cheeses. Today, it isn't uncommon to see anything you can imagine on a pizza, from Swiss chard and roasted duck to grilled apricots and sweet ricotta cheese. The possibilities are endless, not only with the toppings but with the cooking techniques as well.

In this chapter, we explore a broader scope of pizza styles and ingredients. From skillet stuffed pizza to my favorite, grilled pizza, this is a journey through ideas and techniques that will eliminate boring and drab pizza nights for good. To some, calling these "pizzas" may be a stretch, but I like to think of pizza as an icon, a blank canvas where a variety of ingredients, cooking styles, and techniques comes together.

The cooking styles used for contemporary pizzas aren't really all that contemporary—in fact, wood-grilling is a very traditional way for cooking the modern pizza. For convenience, you can cook over a charcoal or gas grill, just as you would grill a steak.

Skillet cooking is a technique that uses a familiar and readily available pan. Cast iron cooking is a more primitive style of cooking that imparts a crisp and delicious crust.

The ingredients and toppings for contemporary pizza are just that: new-world ingredients that are gaining popularity, thus becoming more widely available. This chapter introduces several ingredients that are not typically used on pizzas and explores some interesting and exciting combinations of flavors. Grilling fruit, for example, is one technique that many people are not aware of, yet it is simple to do and the result is a concentrated, flavorful treat that makes an exceptional topping to sweet and savory pizzas.

Salad pizzas are a new-world innovation that gives a more hearty bite to a traditionally "lite" choice. And appetizer pizzas take a familiar form and translate it to tiny, bite-sized servings.

Buffalo Chicken Stuffed-Skillet Pizza

1 round Basic Pizza Dough
(see page 22)

1 pound (225 g) boneless,
skinless chicken breast, cooked
and pulled apart

$\frac{1}{4}$ cup (60 ml) hot sauce

$\frac{1}{3}$ cup (40 g) chopped celery

1 tablespoon (15 ml) olive oil,
plus extra for brushing dough

1 tablespoon (14 g) butter

$\frac{1}{4}$ cup (30 g) crumbled
blue cheese

6 ounces (170 g)
mozzarella cheese

Preheat oven to 450°F (230°C). Heat olive oil and butter in a medium-sized skillet over high heat, then add celery and sauté until tender, about 5 minutes. Remove from heat and set aside.

Oil the bottom and sides of a 10-inch (25-cm) cast-iron or other heavy iron ovenproof skillet. Stretch the dough into a 16-inch (41-cm) circle. Place dough in the skillet, working around bottom and up sides; let excess dough hang over sides of skillet. Drizzle half of the hot sauce on the dough, then top with mozzarella cheese and shredded chicken. Sprinkle with sautéed celery and blue cheese. Drizzle remaining hot sauce over top.

Fold excess pizza dough into pan, covering roughly but not completely. Brush the dough with olive oil. Place on middle rack of oven and cook until dough is browned and crisp, about 45 minutes. Remove from oven and let sit for 5 minutes. Using a sharp knife, slice into wedges and serve.

1 round Basic Pizza Dough
(see page 22), divided

4 eggs

2 tablespoons (30 ml) heavy cream

Salt

Black pepper

2 tablespoons (28 g) butter

6 ounces (170 g) tasso ham or
Canadian bacon, sliced

6 ounces (170 g)
shredded mozzarella cheese

6 ounces (170 g) shredded
fontina cheese

2 tablespoons (8 g)
chopped fresh chives

hollandaise sauce (optional)

Preheat grill to high. Divide dough into four individual balls, then stretch each into an 8-inch (20-cm) thin circle. Brush all circles with olive oil and grill, oil side down, until golden brown, about 4 minutes on each side. Remove from grill and set aside.

Preheat oven to 450°F (230°C) with pizza stone (if using). Whip the eggs with the heavy cream in a mixing bowl, then season with salt and pepper. Melt the butter in a skillet over medium heat, add eggs, and scramble until just beginning to brown, about 4 minutes. (Take care not to overcook the eggs, as they will continue to cook on the pizza.)

Top grilled dough with equal amounts of mozzarella and fontina cheeses, then add sliced ham and eggs. Transfer dough to pizza stone or pan and cook until cheese is melted and starting to brown around the edges, about 10 minutes. Remove from oven and sprinkle with fresh chives and hollandaise sauce (or serve hollandaise on the side). Slice and serve.

[Serves 4]

Brunch Pizza with Scrambled Eggs and Tasso Ham

This brunch pie brings the great flavors of a traditional eggs Benedict to a pizza.

1 round Basic Pizza Dough (see page 22)

Olive oil for brushing dough

6 slices bacon

1/4 pound (115 kg) ground breakfast sausage

1 small red pepper, diced

1 small green pepper, diced

1 small yellow onion, diced

2 tablespoons (20 g) chopped garlic

3 scallions (white and green parts), chopped

4 Roma tomatoes, seeded and sliced thin

5 eggs

2 tablespoons (30 ml) heavy cream

Salt

Fresh ground black pepper

4 ounces (115 g) shredded Monterey jack cheese

6 ounces (170 g) shredded white cheddar cheese (preferably Vermont sharp)

1/4 cup (15 g) cilantro leaves, torn

1 tablespoon (8 g) coarse cornmeal

[Serves 6]

Western Omelet Grilled Pizza

This breakfast or brunch pie combines the great flavors of a traditional western omelet with pizza dough.

Preheat grill to high. Dust peel or pan with cornmeal. Stretch dough into a thin 16-inch (41-cm) rectangle. Oil and grill one side at a time until golden and crisp, about 3 minutes per side. Remove and transfer to pizza peel. Preheat oven to 450°F (230°C) with pizza stone (if using).

Fry bacon over medium-high heat in a large skillet until browned and crisp, about 6 minutes. Transfer to paper towel and let cool, reserving cooking fat. When bacon is cool enough to handle, crumble into small pieces and set aside.

Fry sausage in same skillet until browned, about 6 minutes, then transfer to plate. Clean skillet of drippings. Add two tablespoons (30 ml) bacon fat back to skillet, adjust to medium-high heat, and sauté red and green peppers with onions until just tender, about 3 minutes. Add garlic, scallions, and tomatoes and sauté 3 minutes more, then transfer to plate to cool.

Whip the eggs with the heavy cream in a mixing bowl, then season with salt and pepper. Add 3 additional tablespoons (45 ml) bacon fat to skillet, add eggs, and scramble until tender. Remove and set aside. Top grilled dough with Monterey jack cheese and 4 ounces (115 g) cheddar cheese, then top with pepper/onion mixture, crumbled bacon, sausage, eggs, remaining cheddar cheese, and finally cilantro. Bake on pizza stone or pan until golden and bubbling, about 7 minutes. Remove and let sit for 5 minutes. Slice and serve.

1 round Basic Pizza Dough
(see page 22)

8 ounces (227 g) beef tenderloin

1 tablespoon (6 g) plus
1 teaspoon (2 g) coarse ground
black pepper

2 tablespoons (8 g)
chopped fresh rosemary, divided

8 ounces (225 g) portobello
mushroom caps, stems and gills
removed

1 medium red onion, thinly sliced

1/4 cup (60 ml) Worcestershire
sauce

2 tablespoons (30 ml) olive oil

1 teaspoon (5 ml)
truffle oil (optional)

2 tablespoons (28 g) butter

1/2 cup (120 ml) Madeira wine

1 bulb roasted garlic
(see page 33)

2 tablespoons (10 g)
grated Romano cheese

4 ounces (115 g) Muenster
cheese, thinly sliced

3 scallions, sliced lengthwise

1 tablespoon (8 g)
coarse cornmeal

Preheat oven to 450°F (230°C) with pizza stone (if using). Dust peel or pan with cornmeal. Rub beef tenderloin with 1 tablespoon (6 g) coarse ground black pepper and 1 tablespoon (4 g) rosemary. Toss portobello mushrooms and onions with olive oil and remaining black pepper in a mixing bowl. Coat a roasting pan with nonstick vegetable spray, then place portobello mushrooms and red onions in pan. Set the tenderloin on top of the mushroom/onion mixture and drizzle tenderloin with Worcestershire sauce. Drizzle mushroom/onions mixture with truffle oil and dot with butter. Place pan on middle rack of oven. Cook until internal temperature of the tenderloin reaches 130°F (54°C) and the mushrooms and onions are tender, about 45 minutes; stir mushrooms and onions occasionally. Remove from oven and let tenderloin sit for at least 10 minutes.

Transfer tenderloin to cutting board and slice thin. Transfer mushrooms and onions to a bowl. Add Madeira wine to roasting pan, return to oven and deglaze, scraping pan periodically, to reduce by half. Remove and set aside.

Heat grill to high. Stretch dough into a thin, rough circle and oil one side. Place on grill oiled side down, then oil remaining side and close grill. Cook until browned on both sides. Remove grilled dough and place on pizza peel. Rub generously and evenly with roasted garlic. Sprinkle with Romano and Muenster cheeses, mushroom/onion mixture, and tenderloin. Sprinkle with green onions and rosemary and drizzle with Madeira wine sauce. Place in oven and cook for 30 minutes, or until bubbling and cheese is melted. Remove and let sit for 5 minutes. Slice and serve.

[Serves 4]

Tenderloin and Portobello Mushroom Pizza with Roasted Garlic

The hearty combination of beef and portobello mushrooms brings the flavors of a steakhouse to your table.

1 round Basic Pizza Dough
(see page 22)

2 (8 ounce [225 g]) boneless
skinless chicken breasts,
cooked and cut into large chunks

1/2 cup (120 ml) Thai
peanut satay sauce

3 tablespoons (50 g)
chunky peanut butter

3 tablespoons (45 ml) soy sauce

2 teaspoons (10 ml) sesame oil

1 tablespoon (20 g) honey

1 tablespoon (15 ml)
fresh lime juice

1/2 package thin Asian noodles

Vegetable or peanut oil
for frying

8 ounces (225 g) shredded
mozzarella cheese

1 red pepper, sliced into
thin rings

1/3 cup (40 g) shredded carrot

1/3 cup (40 g) dry
roasted peanuts, chopped

2 scallions, cut into 3-inch
(7.5 cm)-long pieces, then sliced
into thin strips

1/4 cup (15 g) loosely
packed cilantro leaves

1 teaspoon (3 g) coarse cornmeal

Preheat oven to 450°F (230°C) with pizza stone (if using). Combine satay sauce with peanut butter, soy sauce, sesame oil, honey, and lime juice in a mixing bowl. Place the chicken in a second mixing bowl and toss with half of the peanut/satay mixture, then set aside. Heat vegetable oil in a large saucepan to 375°F (190°C). Fry the Asian noodles until golden brown, drain on paper towel, and set aside. Sprinkle cornmeal on pizza peel. Stretch the dough into a 16-inch (41-cm) round, then place on pizza peel and top with remaining peanut/satay sauce and mozzarella, followed by red pepper, carrot, chicken, and peanuts. Transfer pizza to stone and bake until crust is golden, about 15 minutes. Remove from oven, top with scallions, cilantro, and a handful of fried noodles. Slice and serve.

[Serves 4]

Thai Chicken Pizza

This pizza combines traditional Asian flavors and textures. The fried noodles lend a great bite to the dish and also provide a beautiful and artful presentation.

FOR THE ROASTED POTATOES:

1 pound (455 g) (about 3)
Yukon gold potatoes, washed and
cut into 1" (2.5 cm) cubes

2 tablespoons (30 ml) olive oil

2 tablespoons (10 g)
freshly grated Parmesan cheese

2 tablespoons (20 g)
fresh chopped garlic

½ teaspoon (3 g) kosher salt

½ teaspoon (3 g)
coarse ground black pepper

¼ teaspoon (0.5 g)
cayenne pepper

FOR THE PIZZA:

1 round Basic Pizza Dough
(see page 22)

Olive oil for brushing dough

1½ cups (355 ml) Basic
Tomato Sauce (see page 17)

1 cup (80 g) shredded
fontina cheese

¾ cup (85 g) shredded
provolone cheese

2 scallions, sliced into thin strips

1 tablespoon (8 g)
coarse cornmeal

FOR THE SHRIMP:

1 pound (455 g) large shrimp, peeled and deveined

2 tablespoons (30 ml) olive oil

2 tablespoons (30 ml) cider vinegar

1/4 cup (80 g) honey

2 teaspoons (2 g) fresh chopped rosemary

1/2 teaspoon (1 g) coarse ground black pepper

Preheat grill to high. Preheat oven to 375°F (190°C). Combine shrimp with 2 tablespoons (30 ml) olive oil, vinegar, honey, rosemary, and black pepper in a mixing bowl. Cover and refrigerate for at least 30 minutes. In a large cast-iron or other ovenproof skillet, mix potatoes with 2 tablespoons (30 ml) olive oil, Parmesan, garlic, salt, black pepper, and cayenne pepper. Place in oven and bake for about 45 minutes, scraping and stirring every 15 minutes, until golden and tender. In a large skillet over medium-high heat, add 2 tablespoons (30 ml) olive oil, then sauté shrimp until pink and tender. Remove from heat and set aside, reserving pan drippings.

Stretch dough to a thin round. Oil and grill one side at a time until golden and crisp, about 3 minutes per side. Dust peel or pan with cornmeal. Transfer grilled dough to peel. Top grilled dough with tomato sauce, fontina, provolone cheese, sautéed shrimp, and scallions. Transfer pizza to stone and bake until cheese is melted and begins to brown, about 15 minutes. Remove and let sit for 5 minutes, then drizzle with reserved pan drippings. Slice and serve.

[Serves 4]

Pizza **with Rosemary Shrimp and Spicy Golden Potatoes**

Roasted potatoes have a great texture for a pizza; just add cayenne pepper and rosemary-marinated shrimp for an extra bite.

[Serves 4]

Grilled Hoisin Chicken Pizza

The fried wonton strips, which are added
just before serving, make this a special dish.

1 round Basic Pizza Dough
(see page 22)

2 (8-ounce) (225 g))
boneless, skinless chicken breasts

½ cup (120 ml) soy sauce

½ cup (120 ml) orange juice

3 tablespoons (60 g) honey

¼ cup (60 g) Asian hoisin sauce

2 tablespoons (30 g)
whole grain mustard

1 tablespoon (6 g) coarse
ground black pepper

1 tablespoon (8 g)
coarse cornmeal

½ pound (225 g)
fresh asparagus

2 tablespoons (30 ml) olive oil,
plus extra for brushing dough

3 tablespoons (15 g)
grated Parmesan cheese

4 ounces (115 g) shredded
Monterey Jack cheese

4 ounces (115 g) shredded
Vermont sharp white cheddar
cheese

4 ounces (115 g)
shredded mozzarella cheese

3 ounces (85 g) herbed
goat cheese, crumbled

4 ounces (115 g) square wonton
wrappers, cut into thin slices

vegetable oil for frying

Combine soy sauce, orange juice, honey, hoisin, mustard, and black pepper in mixing bowl and stir to combine thoroughly. Set aside ¼ cup (60 ml) marinade mixture. Add the chicken to the remaining marinade mixture, then cover and refrigerate for at least 1 hour or overnight. Preheat grill to high. Preheat oven to 450°F (230°C) with pizza stone (if using). Dust peel or pan with cornmeal. Remove bands from asparagus. Holding one spear in both hands, snap the spear in half; the spear should break where the tough end meets the tender top. Place spears on a platter and drizzle with olive oil. Grill spears until tender and mildly charred all over. Remove, cut into 2-inch (5 cm) lengths, and set aside.

Bring chicken to room temperature and grill until cooked through and browned, about 8 minutes per side. Remove, cut into thin slices, and set aside. Pour enough vegetable oil to fill 2 inches (5 cm) of a medium saucepan. Heat to 375° (190°C), then fry wonton strips in batches until golden, about 2 minutes per batch. Place on paper towel to drain, then set aside.

Stretch dough to a large, thin rectangle. Oil and grill one side at a time until golden and crisp, about 3 minutes per side. Transfer grilled dough to pizza peel or pan. Brush with olive oil, sprinkle with Parmesan, then top with Jack, cheddar, and mozzarella cheeses in even layers. Top with chicken and asparagus, then sprinkle with goat cheese.

Transfer to stone and bake until golden and bubbling, about 15 minutes. Remove from oven, top with fried wonton strips, and drizzle with reserved soy sauce marinade. Slice and serve.

1 round Basic Pizza Dough
(see page 22)

1 pound (455 g) large shrimp,
peeled and deveined

½ cup (120 ml) teriyaki sauce

3 tablespoons (45 ml) soy sauce

2 cloves garlic, minced

1 teaspoon (2 g) fresh
chopped ginger

1 tablespoon (15 ml) Thai hot
chili sauce

2 tablespoons (40 g) honey

Olive oil for brushing dough

1 cup (150 g) red grapes or pear
tomatoes, cut in half lengthwise

2 cups (40 g) bok choy
(or baby bok choy), thinly sliced

8 ounces (225 g)
shredded mozzarella cheese

1 teaspoon (5 ml) fresh lime juice

Preheat oven to 450°F (230°C) with pizza stone (if using). Preheat grill to high. Combine teriyaki sauce, soy sauce, garlic, ginger, hot chili sauce, and honey in a mixing bowl. Add shrimp to marinade and stir to coat, then refrigerate for at least 30 minutes.

Stretch dough to a thin circle. Oil dough on one side and place on hot grill, oiled side down. Oil remaining side, close lid, and grill both sides until browned and crisp. Remove from grill and place on a pizza stone or pan.

Heat 1 tablespoon (15 ml) olive oil in a medium skillet. Transfer shrimp (reserving marinade) to skillet and sauté until pink, turning once, about 5 minutes. Top grilled dough with mozzarella, bok choy, tomatoes, and shrimp, then place in oven and cook until cheese is melted, about 30 minutes. Bring reserved shrimp marinade to a boil in a small saucepan with lime juice; reduce by half. Remove pizza from oven and let rest for 5 minutes. Drizzle with sauce, slice, and serve.

[Serves 4]

Teriyaki Shrimp Grilled Pizza

Teriyaki sauce is a great marinade for anything; just add the bite of Thai chili sauce with crisp bok choy for a superb Asian-inspired pizza.

[Serves 6]

Shitake Mushroom Breakfast Pizza

With a great combination of tasty ingredients, this easy-to-prepare breakfast or brunch pizza is very flavorful and satisfying.

1 round Sweet Pizza Dough
(see page 29)

3 large eggs

1 tablespoon (15 ml) heavy cream

Salt

Black pepper

4 ounces (115 g) pancetta, diced

1 tablespoon (14 g) butter

1 cup (100 g) sliced
shitake mushrooms

1 clove garlic, minced

1 cup (235 ml) Basic Tomato Sauce
(see page 17)

4 ounces (115 g) shredded
mozzarella cheese

4 ounces (115 g) fontina cheese

1 teaspoon (5 ml) truffle oil

1 tablespoon (15 ml) fresh Italian
flat-leaf parsley, chopped

Preheat oven to 450°F (230°C) with pizza stone (if using). Beat the eggs with the heavy cream in a medium mixing bowl, then season with salt and pepper to taste. Brown the pancetta in a medium skillet over medium-high heat until fat is rendered and pancetta is crisp, about 7 minutes. Transfer pancetta to a plate and set aside, leaving drippings in the skillet.

Add butter to the skillet and sauté shitake mushrooms and garlic until tender, about 3 minutes. Remove and set aside. Add beaten eggs to skillet, and scramble about 3 minutes (leave eggs moist, as they will continue to cook on pizza).

Stretch the dough into a 16-inch (41 cm) round. Dust pizza peel with cornmeal. Place stretched dough on peel. Top dough with mozzarella and fontina cheese, add mushroom mixture in even layer, add scrambled eggs, and sprinkle with pancetta.

Transfer to oven and bake until dough is crisp and cheese is bubbling, about 10 minutes. Remove and sprinkle with truffle oil and parsley. Slice and serve.

[Serves 4]

Ciabatta Pizza Loaves

Ciabatta, which is Italian for slipper, is a long, wide loaf of bread. Its soft interior and crisp, thin crust make a great base for any variety of pizza toppings. Its somewhat oily flavor lends itself well to the sausage in this recipe.

1 or 2 loaves ciabatta bread

2 tablespoons (30 ml) olive oil

4 links Italian sausage, cooked, then sliced on the diagonal

1 cup (235 ml) Spicy Tomato Sauce (see recipe, page 18)

6 ounces (170 g) shredded mozzarella cheese

6 leaves ruby Swiss chard, sliced

Preheat oven to 450°F (230°C) with pizza stone (if using). Cut bread loaves in half horizontally, brush cut sides with olive oil, and top with ½ cup (120 ml) tomato sauce per side. Top with mozzarella, Swiss chard, and sausage. Bake until crisp and bubbling, about 10 minutes. Remove and let sit for 5 minutes, then slice and serve.

1 round Basic Pizza Dough
(see page 22)

1 pound (455 g) medium
shrimp, peeled and deveined

1 cup (235 ml) tomato juice

3 tablespoons (45 ml)
Worcestershire sauce

1 tablespoon (15 ml) liquid smoke

3 tablespoons (45 ml)
prepared horseradish

2 tablespoons (30 ml)
fresh lime juice

1 teaspoon (6 g) celery salt

1 1/2 teaspoons (5 g)
garlic powder

1 tablespoon (15 ml) hot sauce

2 tablespoons (30 ml) olive oil

1 (28-ounce [795 g]) can
crushed tomatoes with garlic

1 tablespoon (8 g)
coarse corn meal

6 cloves garlic, peeled
and thinly sliced

vegetable or peanut oil
for frying

6 ounces (170 g) shredded
mozzarella cheese

4 ounces (115 g) shredded
Jack cheese

2 cups (40 g) baby spinach

1 tablespoon (4 g) fresh Italian
flat-leaf parsley, chopped

1/2 cup (120 g) hot banana
pepper rings

2 scallions, thinly sliced

[Serves 4]

Bloody Mary Shrimp Pizza with Fried Garlic

If you enjoy a good, spicy Bloody Mary with its distinctive flavors, you will love this pizza.

Combine tomato juice, Worcestershire sauce, liquid smoke, horseradish, lime juice, celery salt, garlic powder, and hot sauce in large mixing bowl. Add shrimp, toss to coat, cover with plastic wrap, and refrigerate for at least 30 minutes. Preheat oven to 450°F (230°C) with pizza stone (if using). Dust peel or pan with cornmeal. Pour enough vegetable oil to fill 2 inches (5 cm) of a large saucepan. Heat to 375° (190°C), then fry garlic slices until golden brown and crisp, about 4 minutes. Transfer to paper towel to drain and set aside. Heat olive oil in a large skillet over medium-high heat, then add shrimp with some of their juices and sauté until just turning pink, about 5 minutes. Transfer shrimp to a plate; leave juices in skillet. Reduce pan juices by half, then add crushed tomatoes and heat through. Reduce heat to low, simmer for about 5 minutes, then turn off heat and set sauce aside. Stretch dough into a 16-inch (41 cm) round and place on pizza peel. Top dough with tomato sauce, mozzarella, Jack cheese, and spinach, then top with shrimp, pepper rings, and scallions. Transfer to pizza stone and cook until dough is golden and cheese is bubbling, about 10 minutes. Remove from oven, sprinkle with chopped parsley and fried garlic and let sit for 5 minutes. Slice and serve.

1 round Herb Pizza Dough
(see page 26), divided

1 cup (112 g) shredded
mozzarella cheese

3 tablespoons (15 g)
grated Romano cheese

½ cup (120 ml) favorite
marinara sauce

5 ounces (140 g) fresh buffalo
mozzarella cheese, sliced

2 tablespoons (8 g) loosely packed
fresh basil leaves, roughly
chopped or torn

Preheat oven to 450°F (230°C) with pizza stone (if using). Roll dough into a circle measuring 2 inches (5 cm) wider than pizza pan. Place dough on pan with sides overlapping the edge of the pan. Position mozzarella in a 1-inch (2.5 cm) ring around perimeter of pizza pan, then fold excess dough over cheese and press with bottom dough to create a cheese-filled pocket. Press firmly with fingers to ensure a tight seal. Top pizza with Romano cheese and an even layer of marinara and fresh mozzarella, then sprinkle with basil. Brush folded edge of dough with olive oil, then transfer to oven and bake until crust is browned and cheese is bubbling, about 20 minutes. Remove and let sit for 5 minutes. Slice and serve.

[Serves 4]

Marinara and Mozzarella Pizza **with Stuffed Crust**

I recommend using the herb crust with this recipe, but any of the dough recipes will work. Use a good melting cheese in the stuffed crust to ensure lots of gooey goodness.

[Serves 6]

German Sausage and Sauerkraut Pizza with Dark Beer Crust

The flavor of the dark beer crust is a natural choice with sausage and sauerkraut.

1 round Dark Beer Crust
(see page 30)

1 pound (455 g) bratwurst,
grilled and thinly sliced

1 medium white onion, thinly sliced

½ cup (112 g) sauerkraut

8 ounces (225 g) shredded
mozzarella cheese

4 ounces (115 g) shredded
Gruyere cheese

2 tablespoons (30 g)
German-style mustard

¼ cup (60 ml) russian dressing

1 tablespoon (15 ml) olive oil,
plus extra for brushing

1 tablespoon (8 g)
coarse cornmeal

Preheat grill to high. Combine mustard, russian dressing, and olive oil in a small mixing bowl and set aside. Stretch dough into a thin round. Oil and grill one side at a time until golden and crisp, about 3 minutes per side. Dust peel or pan with cornmeal. Remove dough from grill and transfer to pizza peel.

Preheat oven to 450°F (230°C) with pizza stone (if using). Top dough with even layer of the mustard mixture, then add mozzarella, sausage, onion, and sauerkraut and top with Gruyere. Place on pizza stone in oven and bake until golden and bubbling, about 15 minutes. Remove and let sit for 5 minutes. Slice and serve.

Pizza

1 recipe Herbed Pizza Dough
(see page 26)

1 recipe Oven-Dried Tomatoes
(see page 33)

4 tablespoons (60 ml) olive oil
plus extra for brushing dough

1 large eggplant, sliced
lengthwise into ½-inch (1.25 cm)-
thick slices

1 teaspoon (2 g) coarse
ground black pepper

6 ounces (170 g) hummus

2 tablespoons (8 g)
fresh chopped chives, divided

6 ounces (170 g) creamy
Havarti cheese, thinly sliced

4 ounces (115 g) feta cheese,
cut into chunks

1 tablespoon (8 g)
coarse cornmeal

Preheat oven to 450°F (225°C) with stone (if using). Preheat grill to high. Dust peel or pan with cornmeal. Coat the sliced eggplant with 2 tablespoons (30 ml) olive oil, then place on hot grill and cook until browned on both sides, about 5 minutes per side. Remove from grill and let cool. When cool enough to handle, remove skin from sides and cut into large chunks, then set aside. Stretch pizza dough into a 16-inch (41 cm) round. Oil and grill one side at a time until golden and crisp, about 3 minutes per side. Remove from grill and transfer to pizza peel. Combine hummus with 1 tablespoon (15 ml) chives in a small bowl, then spread hummus evenly over grilled dough. Top with Havarti cheese, eggplant, and oven-dried tomatoes, then sprinkle evenly with feta cheese. Transfer to pizza stone and bake until bubbling, about 7 minutes. Remove from oven, sprinkle with remaining chives, and let sit for 5 minutes. Slice and serve.

[Serves 6]

Hummus and Grilled Eggplant Pizza with Feta and Oven-Dried Tomatoes

This Greek-inspired pizza pairs the flavors of hummus and roasted eggplant with chunks of creamy feta cheese and oven-dried tomatoes.

Pizza

Hors d'oeuvres Lavash Pizzas

Lavash bread is a quick and easy
substitute for a pizza shell. Lavash
bread is thin, so limit your toppings to
those without a lot of sauce or moisture.

1 rectangle lavash bread

Olive oil for brushing bread

$1/2$ cup (40 g) shredded fontina cheese

1 Anjou or Bosc pear, peeled, cored, and sliced thin

$1/4$ cup (30 g) crumbled Gorgonzola cheese

1 tablespoon (4 g) fresh tarragon, chopped

1 tablespoon (8 g) coarse cornmeal

Preheat oven to 450°F (230°C) with pizza stone (if using). Dust peel or pan with cornmeal. Place lavash bread on pizza peel, brush with olive oil, then top with fontina cheese, pears, Gorgonzola, and tarragon. Transfer to pizza stone or pan, and bake until golden brown and cheese is bubbling, about 5 minutes. Remove from oven, let sit for 5 minutes, cut into triangles, and serve.

Pear and Gorgonzola with Tarragon

Prosciutto and Basil

1 rectangle lavash bread

Olive oil for brushing bread

$1/2$ cup (55 g) shredded mozzarella cheese

3 slices prosciutto, thinly sliced

freshly ground black pepper

6 fresh basil leaves, torn

1 tablespoon (8 g) coarse cornmeal

Preheat oven to 450°F (230°C) with pizza stone (if using). Dust peel or pan with cornmeal. Place lavash on pizza peel, brush with olive oil, top with mozzarella cheese and prosciutto, and grind fresh black pepper on top. Transfer to pizza stone or pan and bake until golden brown and cheese is bubbling, about 5 minutes. Remove from oven, sprinkle with torn basil leaves, and let sit for 5 minutes. Cut into triangles and serve.

Caramelized Onion and Rosemary with Pancetta

1 rectangle lavash bread

1 tablespoon (15 ml) olive oil, plus extra for brushing bread

3 thick slices pancetta (Italian bacon), diced and fried

1 tablespoon (14 g) butter

1 small Vidalia onion

1 teaspoon (5 g) sugar

1 tablespoon (4 g) fresh rosemary, chopped

1/4 cup (28 g) shredded mozzarella cheese

1/4 cup (40 g) shredded fontina cheese

1 tablespoon (8 g) coarse cornmeal

Preheat oven to 450°F (230°C) with pizza stone (if using). Dust peel or pan with cornmeal. Heat 1 tablespoon (15 ml) olive oil in a skillet over medium-high heat. Add pancetta and fry until crisp and browned, about 7 minutes. Transfer pancetta to paper towel to drain; reserve any drippings in skillet. Add butter to pan, and melt. Sauté onions until just tender, about 3 minutes. Reduce heat to low, add sugar and toss onions to coat, then continue to cook for 5 minutes, stirring occasionally and allowing onions to brown but not crisp. Add rosemary, toss to combine, and cook for 2 more minutes. Remove from heat and let cool.

Place lavash on pizza peel, brush with olive oil, top with mozzarella and fontina cheeses, add caramelized onion mixture evenly over top, and sprinkle with pancetta. Transfer to pizza stone or pan and bake until golden and crisp, about 5 minutes. Remove from oven, let sit for 5 minutes, cut into triangles, and serve.

Pesto, Olive, and Goat Cheese

1 rectangle lavash bread

1/3 cup (78 ml) Basil Pesto (see page 20)

8 ounces (225 g) fresh buffalo mozzarella cheese, thinly sliced

1/4 cup (25 g) oil-cured black olives, pitted and chopped

1/4 cup (40 g) goat cheese, crumbled

1 tablespoon (8 g) coarse cornmeal

Preheat oven to 450°F (230°C) with pizza stone (if using). Dust peel or pan with cornmeal. Place lavash on pizza peel, top evenly with pesto, mozzarella, olives, and goat cheese. Transfer to pizza stone or pan and bake until golden brown and crisp, about 5 minutes. Remove from oven, let sit for 5 minutes, cut into triangles, and serve.

1 round Basic Pizza Dough
(see page 22)

1 cup (235 ml) béchamel
sauce (recipe follows)

8 ounces (225 g)
white cheddar cheese

4 ounces (115 g) baby spinach

8 slices bacon, cooked
and chopped

1 small red onion, chopped

3 ounces (85 g) Jack cheese

8 ounces (225 g) smoked salmon

2 tablespoons (8 g)
fresh chopped chives

1 tablespoon (8 g)
coarse cornmeal

BÉCHAMEL SAUCE:
Makes about 3 cups (700 ml)

3 tablespoons (45 g)
unsalted butter

3 tablespoons (24 g) flour

1 cup (235 ml) dry white wine

1 cup (235 ml) whole milk

1 tablespoon (15 g) Dijon mustard

¼ teaspoon (0.5 g) nutmeg

Salt

White pepper

[For Béchamel Sauce]
In a medium-sized saucepan, scald the milk over medium heat, stirring occasionally, until bubbles form around the sides, then turn off the heat. Melt the butter in a medium-sized skillet over medium-high heat. Add flour and whisk thoroughly to combine. Cook until just turning tan in color, about 3 minutes, stirring constantly. Once roux has reached a light tan color, reduce heat to low, add the white wine, and stir vigorously to incorporate without lumps. Once sauce is thick and wine is incorporated, gradually add scalded milk ⅓ cup (75 ml) at a time, stirring vigorously and continuously between additions to prevent lumps. Add Dijon mustard and nutmeg and season with salt and pepper. The sauce is done when it coats the back of a wooden spoon. If it appears too thick, add more milk.

Preheat grill to high. Preheat oven to 450°F (230°C) with pizza stone (if using). Dust peel or pan with cornmeal.

Stretch dough into a thin 16-inch (41 cm) round. Oil and grill both sides until golden, about 3 minutes per side. Transfer to pizza pan or peel, top with béchamel sauce, Cheddar cheese, spinach, bacon, onion, and Jack cheese, then finish with salmon. Bake until golden and bubbling, about 10 minutes. Remove, sprinkle with chives, and let sit 5 minutes. Slice and serve.

[Serves 4]

Pizza **Montréal**

On a recent visit to Montreal, I ate my way through most of the city. I developed this recipe based on the ingredients and flavors I encountered there.

1 round Basic Pizza Dough
(see page 22), divided

1/4 cup (60 ml) extra virgin olive
oil for brushing and drizzling

1/2 teaspoon (1.5 g)
minced fresh garlic

1/2 cup (4 g) shredded fontina
cheese, loosely packed

2 tablespoons (10 g) freshly
grated Pecorino Romano cheese

6 tablespoons (90 g) chopped,
canned tomatoes, in heavy puree

fried calamari (recipe follows)

Hot Pepper–Infused Olive Oil
(recipe follows)

8 basil leaves

1 tablespoon (8 g)
coarse cornmeal

FOR FRIED CALAMARI:

5 ounces (140 g) fresh calamari,
tubes and tentacles cleaned

1 cup (110 g) all-purpose flour

1/4 cup (18 g) semolina flour

1/2 teaspoon (1 g) coarse ground
black pepper

vegetable or peanut oil for frying

FOR HOT PEPPER–INFUSED
OLIVE OIL:

3 cups (700 ml) olive oil

1/4 cup (28 g) hot paprika

1/4 cup (28 g) crushed
red pepper flakes

3 garlic cloves, peeled
and trimmed

[For fried calamari]
Pour enough vegetable oil to
fill 2 inches (5 cm) of a medium
saucepan. Heat to 360°F
(180°C). Cut calamari tubes
into rings, then combine flour,
semolina, and pepper in a bowl.
Lightly coat calamari with flour
mixture and fry until golden
brown. Remove and set aside.

**[For hot pepper–infused
olive oil]**
Combine all ingredients in a
heavy saucepan. Bring to a
boil, then lower heat to very
low and simmer gently for
10 minutes. Remove from heat
and set aside for 30 minutes
for flavors to infuse. Strain the
oil into a clean jar. Once cooled
to room temperature, cover
and refrigerate.

Preheat grill to high. Preheat
oven to 450°F (230°C) with
pizza stone (if using). Dust peel
or pan with cornmeal. On a
large, oiled, inverted baking
sheet, spread and flatten the
dough into a 10- to 12-inch
(25–30 cm) free-form circle,
1/8 -inch (0.3 cm) thick. The final
shape is not as important as
maintaining an even thickness.
Brush dough with olive oil.
Place dough on grill, cook for
about 2 minutes, and flip over
using tongs. Continue to grill
until crisp, about 2 more
minutes, then transfer to pizza
pan or peel. Brush grilled
surface with olive oil, scatter
the garlic and cheese, and
finish with dollops of tomatoes.
(Do not cover the entire surface
of the pizza with tomatoes.)
Drizzle with 1 to 2 tablespoons
(15 to 30 ml) hot pepper oil.
Bake until bubbling and
browned, about 10 minutes.
Remove and top with fried
calamari, scallions, and basil.
Slice and serve.

[Serves 4]

Grilled Pizza with Fried Calamari

It is said that Johanne Killeen and George Germon of
Al Forno restaurant in Providence, Rhode Island, are the
original creators of grilled pizza. This recipe is adapted
from a recipe in their book *Cucina Simpatica*.

1 round Basic Pizza Dough (see page 22)

3 ears fresh corn, shucked

4 tablespoons (55 g) butter, divided

2 tablespoons (20 g) chopped fresh garlic, divided

Salt

½ teaspoon (1 g) black pepper, plus extra for seasoning

1 (10-ounce [280 g]) can black beans, drained

1 small red pepper, diced

3 tablespoons (45 ml) olive oil, divided

1 teaspoon (3 g) chili powder

½ teaspoon (1 g) cayenne pepper

½ teaspoon (1.5 g) onion powder

1 pound (455 g) large shrimp, peeled and deveined

1 tablespoon (9 g) ancho chili powder

1 teaspoon (3 g) garlic powder

1 teaspoon (2 g) ground cumin

1 teaspoon (2 g) ground coriander

2 teaspoons (10 ml) hot sauce

1 tablespoon (8 g) coarse cornmeal

4 ounces (115 g) shredded Jack cheese

6 ounces (170 g) shredded monchego cheese

¼ cup (15 g) fresh cilantro, coarsely chopped

Black Bean and Roasted Corn Pizza with Seared Shrimp and Monchego Cheese

Black beans are a great addition to any Spanish- or Mexican-inspired dish, and they are also good for you. This recipe pairs them with grill-roasted corn and pan-seared shrimp for a spectacular combination of flavors.

Preheat grill to high. Preheat oven to 450°F (230°C) with pizza stone (if using). Dust peel or pan with cornmeal. Tear three sheets of aluminum foil large enough to wrap the corn cobs completely. Place one ear of corn on each piece of foil, top with equal amounts butter and garlic, and season generously with salt and pepper. Wrap foil by bringing front and back together and rolling down towards the cob; keep a loose fit (like a tent) at the top, then fold in the sides tightly. Place corn on grill, reduce heat to medium, close lid, and grill corn for about 15 to 20 minutes, turning every 5 minutes. Remove from grill, open foil packets, and set aside to cool.

Toss the shrimp with ancho chili powder, garlic powder, cumin, coriander, hot sauce, and $\frac{1}{2}$ teaspoon (1 g) black pepper in a mixing bowl, coating evenly. Heat 2 tablespoons (30 ml) olive oil in large skillet over medium-high heat. Saute shrimp in skillet until just pink, but still tender, about 5 minutes; do not overcook. Transfer to bowl and set aside.

Stand corn cob on end on cutting board and cut away the kernels, holding the corn cob upright with one hand.

Repeat with remaining two cobs, then place corn kernels in a mixing bowl. Add black beans, red pepper, remaining olive oil, cayenne pepper, and onion powder to corn kernels, toss to combine, and set aside. Stretch the dough into a 16-inch (41 cm) round. Place dough on peel, then top with even layers of shredded Jack and monchego cheese, followed by black bean and corn mixture and seared shrimp. Transfer to pizza stone or pan and bake until golden and cheese is bubbling, about 7 minutes. Remove from oven, top with cilantro, and let sit for 5 minutes. Slice and serve.

chapter 6

Salad Pizza

A truly modern take on pizza is to forgo the side order of salad and simply put it on top of a delicious, cheesy pie. Throughout this chapter, I have tried to pair some traditional flavors and concepts with some new ideas. These recipes are very easy to assemble; you can make a large pizza to serve a group, or shrink the crusts to individual size and serve a small tossed salad on top for lunch or appetizer.

1 round Basic Pizza Dough
(see page 22)

olive oil for brushing dough

1 ½ cups (355 ml)
Basil Pesto (see page 20)

¼ cup (20 g) grated
Parmesan cheese

8 ounces (225 g)
shredded mozzarella cheese

1 (8-ounce [225 g]) boneless,
skinless chicken breast,
cooked and shredded

1 small head romaine
lettuce, chopped

1 cup (60 g) Garlic
Croutons (recipe follows)

6 slices good-quality,
thick-cut bacon, cooked and
crumbled

⅓ cup (75 ml) Caesar
Dressing (recipe follows)

GARLIC CROUTONS:
Makes about 2 cups (120 g)

1 day-old loaf French bread, cut into 1-inch (2.5 cm) cubes

2 tablespoons (20 g) fresh chopped garlic

1 tablespoon (15 g) Italian seasoning

1/2 teaspoon (3 g) kosher salt

1/4 teaspoon (0.5 g) coarse ground black pepper

3 tablespoons (40 g) butter, melted

CAESAR DRESSING:
Makes about 1 1/2 cups (350 ml)

1 tablespoon (15 g) mayonnaise

1 teaspoon (5 g) Dijon mustard

2 cloves fresh garlic, finely chopped

1 teaspoon (6 g) kosher salt

4 anchovy fillets (optional)

1 teaspoon (5 g) lemon zest

1/4 cup (60 ml) freshly squeezed lemon juice (about 1 large lemon)

1/4 teaspoon (0.5 g) coarse ground black pepper

3/4 cup (175 ml) mild olive oil

1/4 cup (60 ml) freshly grated Parmigiano-Reggiano cheese

[For garlic croutons]

Preheat oven to 350° F (180°C). Place bread, garlic, Italian seasoning, salt, and black pepper in a mixing bowl, then toss to combine. Drizzle with butter and toss vigorously to coat evenly. Transfer to a baking sheet and place on middle rack of oven. Bake until browned and crisp, about 45 minutes; stir and rotate pan every 15 minutes. Remove and let cool. Use immediately or place in an airtight container and store for up to 1 week.

[For caesar dressing]

Combine mayonnaise, mustard, garlic, salt, anchovies, lemon zest, lemon juice, and black pepper in the bowl of a food processor fitted with the blade attachment. Pulse until well combined, then, with motor running, add olive oil in a steady stream, blending to emulsify. Remove and stir in Parmigiano-Reggiano cheese. Cover and refrigerate until ready to use.

Preheat grill to high. Preheat oven to 450°F (230°C) with pizza stone (if using). Stretch dough into a thin round. Oil and grill one side at a time until golden and crisp, about 3 minutes per side. Transfer to a pizza stone or pan. Top with basil pesto, Parmesan, and mozzarella cheese. Place in oven or on stone and bake until cheese is melted and begins to brown, about 15 minutes. Remove and let rest for 5 minutes. Meanwhile, combine chicken, romaine lettuce, croutons, and bacon in large mixing bowl, then toss with Caesar dressing. Top pizza with salad. Slice and serve.

[Serves 4]

Chicken Caesar Salad Pizza

Caesar salad, probably one of the most traditional and easily recognized salads, works well atop grilled pizza dough with melted cheese.

3 fresh garlic cloves

1 1/2 teaspoons (9 g)
kosher salt

1 1/2 teaspoons (5 g) paprika

1 1/2 teaspoons (3 g)
ground cumin

1 1/2 teaspoons (3 g)
ground coriander

1 teaspoon (2 g) coarse
ground black pepper

1 tablespoon (15 g)
Dijon mustard

2 tablespoons (30 ml) canola oil

2 dashes hot sauce

1 1/4 pound (0.6 kg) skirt steak

1 round Basic Pizza Dough
(see page 22)

olive oil for rubbing steak

8 ounces (225 g) shredded
fontina cheese

6 ounces (170 g) shredded
Gruyere cheese

4 ounces (115 g) mixed
salad greens

2 ounces (55 g) baby spinach

3 tablespoons (12 g)
chopped fresh chives

1/4 cup (5 g) loosely packed
fresh basil leaves, roughly
chopped or torn

1/4 cup (5 g) loosely packed fresh
Italian flat-leaf parsley, roughly
chopped or torn

1/4 cup (60 ml) prepared
balsamic vinaigrette dressing

1/4 cup (20 g) shaved
Parmigiano-Reggiano cheese

In a small bowl, mash garlic and salt to form a paste. Combine paprika, cumin, coriander, and black pepper in small skillet and toast over medium heat, stirring constantly until aromatic, about 3 minutes. Transfer to medium mixing bowl and add garlic paste, Dijon mustard, oil, and hot sauce. Stir to combine. Rub mixture over skirt steak, working it into the meat, then cover with plastic wrap and refrigerate for at least 6 hours or overnight.

Bring steak to room temperature while preheating grill to high. Soak mesquite wood chips in water, fully submerged, for at least 30 minutes. If using a charcoal grill, prepare and light coals. Sprinkle moist wood chips over charcoal. If using a gas grill, preheat to high for 10 minutes, then reduce to medium. Place moist wood chips into a fire box and place to one side of grill. Once wood chips are smoking, lightly oil the grill grates and grill steak, turning only once, until medium rare, about 7 minutes on each side.

Meanwhile, toss mixed greens and spinach with fresh herbs and vinaigrette. Stretch dough into a rough circle and oil one side. Remove steak from grill and set aside for about 5 minutes. Clean grill grates, then place dough on hot grill, oiled side down. Oil remaining side, then close grill and cook until golden and crisp, about 3 minutes. Reduce heat to low, flip over dough, and top with fontina and gruyere cheese. Grill until cheese is melted. Remove and let sit. Cut steak diagonally against the grain into 1/4-inch (1.3 cm) thick slices. Place greens atop grilled cheese pizza and top with skirt steak and shaved Parmigiano-Reggiano. Slice and serve.

[Serves 4]

Fontina and Gruyere Pizza Shell with Skirt Steak Salad

The rub used on this steak is very tasty and can also be used on chicken and seafood.

[Serves 4]

Ancho-Seared Shrimp and Spicy Caesar Pizza

Ancho chili powder is a unique dried, ground chili with a smoky flavor that works well with shrimp.

1 round Basic Pizza Dough (see page 22)

1 pound (455 g) large shrimp, peeled and deveined

1 tablespoon (9 g) dried ancho chili powder

1/2 teaspoon (1 g) coarse ground black pepper

3 tablespoons (45 ml) canola oil

Olive oil for brushing dough

8 ounces (225 g) shredded mozzarella cheese

1/4 cup (60 ml) shredded Asiago cheese

6 ounces (170 g) shaved Parmigiano-Reggiano cheese, divided

1 head romaine lettuce, chopped

1/4 cup (5 g) fresh arugula leaves, torn

1/4 cup (5 g) fresh cilantro leaves, roughly chopped

1/4 cup (60 ml) Caesar Dressing (see page 107, or use favorite bottled brand)

2 chipotle peppers in adobo sauce, chopped

1 tablespoon (8 g) coarse cornmeal

Preheat grill to high. Preheat oven to 450°F (230°C) with pizza stone (if using). Combine shrimp with ancho chili powder, pepper, and 2 tablespoons canola oil in mixing bowl, toss, then cover and refrigerate for at least 30 minutes.

Stretch dough to a thin round. Oil and grill one side at a time until golden and crisp, about 3 minutes per side. Dust pizza peel with cornmeal. Transfer grilled dough to pizza peel. Top with mozzarella and Asiago cheeses and half of Parmigiano-Reggiano cheese. Transfer to stone and bake until cheese is melted and begins to brown, about 15 minutes. Remove and let rest.

Meanwhile, heat remaining canola oil over medium-high heat in medium-sized skillet, add shrimp and sear on each side until pink. Remove from heat and let cool. In a small mixing bowl, combine Caesar dressing with chipotle peppers, then cover and refrigerate. In a large mixing bowl, combine romaine lettuce, arugula, and cilantro, and toss with Caesar dressing. Add shrimp and toss again. Top pizza with shrimp salad, slice and serve.

1 round Basic Pizza Dough (see page 22)

Olive oil

1 zucchini, sliced lengthwise into 1/2-inch (1 cm)-thick slices

1 squash, sliced lengthwise into 1/2-inch (1 cm)-thick slices

1 eggplant, sliced lengthwise into 1/2-inch (1 cm)-thick slices

1 red onion, sliced in half and then into thick slices

2 large carrots, peeled and sliced lengthwise into thick slices

2 portabella mushrooms, stems removed

8 ounces (225 g) shredded Monterey Jack cheese

4 ounces (115 g) grated Parmesan cheese

6 ounces (170 g) mixed greens (such as mesclun mix)

6 ounces (170 g) crumbled feta cheese

1/2 cup (120 ml) Balsamic Vinaigrette (recipe follows)

PARMESAN BALSAMIC VINAIGRETTE:
Makes about 1 cup (235 ml)

2 cloves garlic, minced

1/2 teaspoon (3 g) salt

2 tablespoons (28 ml) balsamic vinegar

1 teaspoon (5 ml) fresh lemon juice

3 tablespoons (12 g) minced fresh basil

1/4 cup (20 g) finely grated Parmesan cheese

1/4 teaspoon (0.5 g) coarse ground black pepper

1/2 cup (120 ml) extra-virgin olive oil

[For parmesan balsamic vinaigrette]
Mash the garlic and salt together in a small bowl to form a paste. Using a whisk, combine the garlic paste with the balsamic vinegar, lemon juice, basil, Parmesan cheese, and black pepper. Add oil in a steady stream while whisking to emulsify.

Preheat outdoor grill to high heat. Place sliced zucchini, squash, eggplant, onions, and carrots in a large mixing bowl or platter. Drizzle with olive oil and toss to coat. Do the same with the whole mushroom caps. Grill

[Serves 4]

Grilled Vegetable Salad Pizza with Parmesan Balsamic Vinaigrette

Grilling vegetables may be the most flavorful way of cooking them. Toss them with vinaigrette and greens, for a great beginning to any meal.

vegetables on hot grill for about 4 minutes on each side, until tender and browned. The mushroom caps will probably need about 6 minutes on each side. Remove vegetables from grill and set aside to cool. When the vegetables are cool enough to handle, chop them all, including the mushroom caps, into cubes. Set aside.

Meanwhile, stretch the pizza dough into a thin, roughly rectangular shape about 18" × 12" (45 × 30 cm). Place on a large baking sheet and oil one side. Let rest while grill heats. Place dough on hot grill, oil side down, and let cook for about 3 minutes, until dough begins to rise and is crisp on the cooking side. Oil the uncooked side and flip dough over. Reduce heat to low. Sprinkle dough with Parmesan and Monterey cheese, evenly distributing the cheese around the dough. Cook until cheese is melted. Remove from heat and set aside.

To prepare salad, in a large mixing bowl, combine the chopped grilled vegetables, salad greens, and feta cheese. Toss with balsamic dressing. Serve salad mixture over grilled pizza crust, cutting into individual serving portions. When eating, fold dough in half over topping, like a sandwich.

Pizza

1 round Basic Pizza Dough
(see page 22)

olive oil for brushing dough

6 ounces (170 g) mixed
salad greens

6 ounces (170 g) snow peas,
sliced into thin strips

1 red pepper, sliced into
thin strips

1 yellow pepper, sliced into
thin strips

2 large carrots, shredded

1 cup (70 g) shredded
Chinese cabbage

6 ounces (170 g) square
wonton wrappers

Vegetable oil for frying

1/3 cup (75 ml) Sesame
Ginger Dressing (recipe follows)

8 ounces (225 g) shredded
white sharp cheddar cheese

4 ounces (115 g) shredded
Asiago cheese

SESAME GINGER DRESSING:
Makes about 1 cup (235 ml)

1 tablespoon (15 ml) tahini paste

1 tablespoon (15 ml) sesame oil

1 teaspoon (2.5 g) toasted
sesame seeds

1/4 cup (60 ml) canola oil

1 teaspoon (5 g) packed
brown sugar

1 tablespoon (7 g) fresh
chopped ginger

1 clove garlic, minced

1 tablespoon (15 ml) soy sauce

[For sesame ginger dressing]
Combine tahini paste, sesame oil, brown sugar, ginger, garlic, and soy sauce in a blender or the bowl of a food processor fitted with the blade attachment, then pulse to combine. With motor running, slowly add canola oil in a steady stream to emulsify. Transfer to container, add sesame seeds, and refrigerate for at least 30 minutes.

Preheat grill to high. Stretch dough out into a thin rectangle. Rub one side of dough with olive oil and place oiled side down on hot grill, then oil remaining side. Cook on medium-high heat, until golden, about 3 minutes. Turn dough and top with cheeses, reduce heat to low, cover, and continue to grill until cheese is melted. Remove and let sit for 5 minutes.

Combine salad greens, snow peas, red and yellow peppers, carrots, and cabbage in large mixing bowl, then toss to combine. Drizzle with dressing and toss to coat just before ready to serve. Heat about 2 inches (5 cm) vegetable oil in a large saucepan to 375°F (190°C). Cut wonton squares into 4 wedges. Fry in hot oil until crisp and browned. Remove and let drain. Toss wontons with salad, then place salad on top of cheese pizza. Slice and serve.

[Serves 4]

Asian Salad Grilled Pizza

Asian-inspired flavors are unique and refreshing. Asian cooking offers so many great ingredients to choose from—don't be afraid to experiment!

chapter 7

Sweet Pizza

My first taste of sweet pizza was basically an apple pie atop a tender, chewy, cinnamon-scented pizza crust. What a pleasant surprise—something better than pepperoni and sausage pizza with extra cheese! The following recipes for sweet pizza combine fresh fruit with traditional Italian cheeses.

Mixed Berries on Grilled Pizza Shell with Mascarpone Spread

Pizza crust used as a dessert base is just as good as any tart or pie shell. Pile high with berries and sweet mascarpone cheese for an excellent, sweet temptation.

1 round Sweet Pizza Dough (see page 29)

16 ounces (455 gm) mascarpone cheese

4 ounces (115 g) cream cheese, room temperature

1/4 cup (30 g) sifted powdered sugar

1 tablespoon (7 g) ground cinnamon

1 teaspoon (2 g) ground nutmeg

1 teaspoon (5 ml) vanilla extract

1 teaspoon (5 ml) lemon extract

1 tablespoon lemon zest

2 tablespoons (40 g) honey

1 pint (300 g) strawberries, washed, hulled, and sliced in half

1 pint (300 g) red raspberries

1 pint (300 g) blackberries

1/2 pint (150 g) blueberries (optional)

1/2 cup (120 ml) strawberry glaze (recipe follows)

powdered sugar, for garnish

fresh mint, for garnish

STRAWBERRY GLAZE:

1 pint (300 g) strawberries, stemmed and chopped

1 tablespoon (15 ml) water

1/4 cup (30 g) granulated sugar

(continued on next page)

(continued from previous page)

Preheat grill to medium-high heat. Stretch pizza dough into a moderately thin round. Dust a pizza peel with flour or corn meal. Place the stretched pizza dough on the peel and oil one side. Place dough on heated grill, oil side down. Cook for about 3 minutes, until dough is browned and crisp. Oil top of dough and flip. Continue to cook for about 3 more minutes. Remove from grill and set aside to cool.

To prepare the mascarpone spread, in a small mixing bowl combine the mascarpone cheese, cream cheese, powdered sugar, cinnamon, nutmeg, vanilla extract, lemon extract, lemon zest, and honey. Whip until smooth. Spread cheese mixture evenly on grilled pizza crust, leaving about a 1-inch (2.5 cm) clean border around crust. Top with an artful arrangement of mixed berries with strawberries forming an outer ring and working in toward the center, finishing with raspberries in the center. Brush berries with strawberry glaze. Chill dessert for at least 1 hour. Sprinkle with powdered sugar and garnish with mint. Cut to serve.

[For the strawberry glaze]

Makes $^1/_2$ cup (115 ml)

Place all ingredients in a medium-sized saucepan. Bring to a boil to dissolve sugar. Reduce heat to a simmer. Continue to cook, stirring occasionally, until strawberries are cooked down and sauce is thickened, about 15 minutes. Remove from heat and pass through a medium gauge strainer into a bowl, using a rubber spatula to press against the sides of the strainer. Discard the pulp. Makes about $^1/_2$ cup (120 ml) sauce.

FOR THE PIZZA:

1 frozen puff pastry sheet (from a 17¼-ounce [490 g] package), thawed

2 tablespoons (12 g) ginger snap or graham cracker crumbs

1½ tablespoons (20 g) unsalted butter

1½ pounds (0.7 kg) (3 medium) Golden Delicious apples, peeled, halved lengthwise, cored, and thinly sliced crosswise

¼ cup (60 g) sugar

¼ teaspoon (0.5 g) cinnamon

⅛ teaspoon (0.7 g) salt

1 egg

1 tablespoon (15 ml) water

1 cup (120 g) grated sharp white cheddar cheese

FOR THE CRUMBLE:

4 tablespoons butter (56 g), softened

½ cup (35 g) oats

1 tablespoon (14 g) packed brown sugar

½ teaspoon (1 g) ground cinnamon

¼ teaspoon (0.5 g) nutmeg

⅛ teaspoon (0.25 g) ground cloves

¼ cup (31 g) chopped pecans

FOR THE SWEET VANILLA DRIZZLE:

¼ cup (25 g) confectioners' (powdered) sugar, sifted

2 tablespoons (30 ml) milk

¼ teaspoon (1.3 ml) vanilla

Preheat oven to 450°F (230°C) with rack in middle. Roll out pastry sheet into 15" x 12" (38 x 30 cm) rectangle on a lightly floured surface using a flour-dusted rolling pin. Transfer to a baking sheet lined with parchment paper, then prick with a fork to prevent bubbling during baking.

Sprinkle ginger snap (or graham cracker) crumbs over dough. Heat butter in a small saucepan over medium heat until golden brown, about 2 minutes, swirling constantly. Pour butter over apples in a mixing bowl, add sugar and salt, and toss lightly to coat. Layer apples evenly over pastry, leaving a 1-inch (2.5 cm) border around the perimeter. Fold in edges over the apples, pressing down firmly on the corners and sides. In a small bowl, whisk egg and water. Brush the edges and sides of pastry with the egg wash using a pastry brush. Place pastry in oven and bake until apples are tender and pastry is golden, about 35 to 40 minutes.

To make crumble topping, place butter in a small mixing bowl and add brown sugar, oats, pecans, cinnamon, nutmeg, and cloves. Using your fingers or a fork, work the mixture until achieving a chunky, crumbled texture.

For the drizzle, combine confectioners' sugar, milk, and vanilla in a small mixing bowl, then stir to combine thoroughly. Remove pizza from oven, sprinkle with cheese and crumble topping, and bake for an additional 6 to 9 minutes or until cheese is melted and topping is browned. Using a fork or a plastic sandwich bag with a tiny hole cut in one corner, drizzle the pizza with Sweet Vanilla Drizzle. Slice and serve warm.

[Serves 6]

Apple Crumble "Pizza"

This recipe uses puff pastry for the crust. The combination of apples, crumble topping, cheddar cheese, and a sweet vanilla drizzle makes a perfect pizza for dessert or brunch.

[Serves 6]

Apricot and Blackberry Pizza with Camembert and Sweet Ricotta Cheese

Fresh summer apricots are great on their own, but they are simply superb when combined with blackberries and sweetened ricotta cheese.

1 round Sweet Pizza Dough
(see page 29)

olive oil for brushing dough

½ cup (160 g) apricot preserves

6 apricots, peeled and sliced

½ pint (130 g) fresh blackberries

4 ounces (115 g)
Camembert cheese, cut into
thick slices

Sweet Ricotta Cheese
(recipe follows)

Preheat grill to high. Stretch dough to a large rectangular shape. Oil and grill one side at a time until golden and crisp, about 3 minutes per side. Transfer to pizza pan and let cool. Preheat oven broiler. Heat apricot preserves in a small saucepan over low heat. Spread apricot preserves over top of grilled dough, then top with Sweet Ricotta cheese. Arrange apricots and blackberries over ricotta cheese and top with Camembert. Place under broiler to melt and brown the cheese, about 4 minutes— careful not to burn. Remove, slice, and serve.

SWEET RICOTTA CHEESE:
1/2 cup (115 g) ricotta cheese

2 tablespoons (40 g) honey

3 tablespoons (20 g)
powdered sugar

1/8 teaspoon (0.25 g) nutmeg

Combine all ingredients in a
small mixing bowl. Cover and
refrigerate until ready to use.

1 round Chocolate Pizza
Dough (see page 28)

1 (8-ounce [225 g]) container
mascarpone cheese, softened

2 tablespoons (12 g)
powdered sugar

2 tablespoons (40 g) honey

½ teaspoon (2.5 ml) vanilla
extract

1 tablespoon (15 ml) orange
liqueur (such as Grand Marnier)

2 tablespoons (30 ml)
orange marmalade

2 pints (600 g) large strawberries,
washed, dried, and tops removed

1 mango, peeled and sliced
into thin strips

Cabernet Chocolate Sauce
(recipe follows)

CABERNET CHOCOLATE SAUCE:
Makes about 1 cup (235 ml)

½ cup (120 ml) heavy cream

8 ounces (225 g) semi-sweet
chocolate, finely chopped

1 tablespoon (15 ml)
Cabernet Sauvignon

Preheat grill to high. Stretch dough into a roughly rectangular shape about 16" x 24" (41 x 61 cm). Oil and grill one side at a time until toasted, about 3 minutes per side. Let cool. Combine mascarpone cheese with sugar, honey, vanilla, orange liqueur, and orange marmalade in a mixing bowl, then stir to combine. Cut strawberries in half from top to bottom, then place in a bowl and toss with 1 tablespoon (15 ml) olive oil. Grill for about 4 minutes, turning each berry as they cook. (Take care not to overcook the strawberries, as they will become too soft and difficult to handle.) Remove strawberries from grill and transfer to a bowl. Spread mascarpone cheese mixture evenly over the top of the grilled pizza dough. Top with strawberries and mango in an artful manner. Slice and place on serving plates. Using a fork or a plastic sandwich bag with a tiny hole cut in one corner, drizzle the slices with chocolate sauce and serve.

[For cabernet chocolate sauce]
Heat heavy cream in a saucepan over medium heat just until foaming and bubbles begin to form around the sides. Add chocolate and swirl to melt and combine with cream. Turn off heat and add wine, then swirl to combine. Cover and set aside until ready to use.

[Serves 6]

Grilled Strawberry and Mango Chocolate Pizza

For a truly exceptional dessert pizza, this one hits the mark. Grilling strawberries concentrates and adds a smoky bite to their flavor.

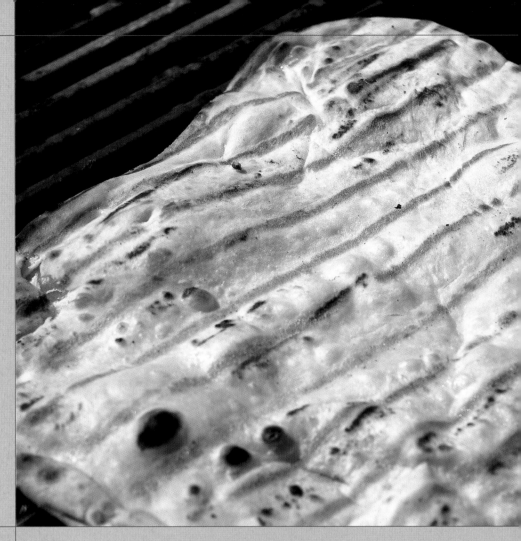

Index

A

Ancho-Seared Shrimp and Spicy Caesar Pizza, 111
Apple Crumble "Pizza," 119
Appliances, 37
Apricot and Blackberry Pizza with Camembert and Sweet Ricotta Cheese, 120–121
Asian Salad Grilled Pizza, 115
Asparagus
  Grilled Asparagus and Cheese Pizza with White Truffle Oil, 56–57
  Grilled Hoisin Chicken Pizza, 82–83

B

Basil
  Basil Pesto Pizza Dough, 31
  Pesto and Black Olive Pizza, 61
  Prosciutto and Basil, 98
  Proven Basil Pesto, 20–21
Béchamel Sauce, 100
Beef
  Fontina and Gruyere Pizza Shell with Skirt Steak Salad, 108–109
  Individual Grilled Greek-Style Pizza, 58–59
  Meatball and Tomato Stew Grilled Pizza, 44–45
  New York-Style Stone-Baked Pizza, 54–55
  Tenderloin and Portobello Mushroom Pizza with Roasted Garlic, 77
Beer Crust, Dark, 30
Berries
  Apricot and Blackberry Pizza with Camembert and Sweet Ricotta Cheese, 120–121
  Mixed Berries on Grilled Pizza Shell with Mascarpone Spread, 117–118
Black Bean and Roasted Corn Pizza with Seared Shrimp and Monchego Cheese, 102–103
Bread, 32
Breakfast/brunch pizzas
  Brunch Pizza with Scrambled Eggs and Tasso Ham, 75
  Shitake Mushroom Breakfast Pizza, 86–87
  Western Omelet Grilled Pizza, 76
Brick ovens, 37
Broccoli Rabe, Pizza Bianca with Roasted Garlic, Ricotta, and, 64–65
Buffalo Chicken Stuffed-Skillet Pizza, 72

C

Cabbage
  Asian Salad Grilled Pizza, 115
Calamari, Grilled Pizza with Fried, 101
Calzone, Deli Counter, 67
Cast iron skillets, 37
Cheese, 13–14. see also specific types
Cheesiest Cheesy and Herb Pizza, 49
Chicago-Style Deep Dish Pizza, 62
Chicken
  BBQ Chicken Pizza with Smoked Gouda and Grilled Pineapples, 43
  Buffalo Chicken Stuffed-Skillet Pizza, 72
  Chicken Caesar Salad Pizza, 106–107
  Garlic-Grilled Chicken and Pepperoni Pizza with Smoked Gouda, 53
  Grilled Hoisin Chicken Pizza, 82–83
  Thai Chicken Pizza, 78
  Wood-Grilled Chicken Pizza with Radicchio and Feta, 46
  Ziti Pizza with Citrus Chicken and Mozzarella, 68
Chickpeas
  Hummus and Grilled Eggplant Pizza with Feta and Oven-Dried Tomatoes, 95
Chocolate
  Cabernet Chocolate Sauce, 123
  Chocolate Pizza Dough, 28
  Grilled Strawberries and Mango Chocolate Pizza, 123
Ciabatta Pizza Loaves, 88–89
Cilantro Mint Pesto, 58–59
Clam and Roasted Garlic Thin-Crust Pizza, 69
Cooking techniques, 35–36
Corn Pizza with Seared Shrimp and Monchego Cheese, Black Bean and Roasted, 102–103
Crust types, 11. see also dough

D

Deep-Dish Pizza, Chicago-Style, 62
Dessert pizzas. see Sweet pizzas
Dough
  alternatives to, 32
  Basic Pizza Dough, 22–23
  Basil Pesto Pizza Dough, 31
  Chocolate Pizza Dough, 28
  Dark Beer Crust, 30
  freezing, 23
  Herbed Pizza Dough, 26
  ingredients, 11–12

No Oil Neapolitan-Style Pizza Dough, 24
  premade, 32
  Sweet Pizza Dough, 29
  Whole Wheat and Honey Pizza Dough, 25

E

Eggplant
  Grilled Vegetable Salad Pizza with Balsamic Vinaigrette, 112–113
  Hummus and Grilled Eggplant Pizza with Feta and Oven-Dried Tomatoes, 95
  Individual Grilled Greek-Style Pizza, 58–59
Eggs
  Brunch Pizza with Scrambled Eggs and Tasso Ham, 75
  Shitake Mushroom Breakfast Pizza, 86–87
  Western Omelet Grilled Pizza, 76

F

Feta cheese
  Cheesiest Cheesy and Herb Pizza, 49
  Hummus and Grilled Eggplant Pizza with Feta and Oven-Dried Tomatoes, 95
  Individual Grilled Greek-Style Pizza, 58–59
  Roasted Wild Mushroom Pizza with Pancetta and Feta, 50–51
  Wood-Grilled Chicken Pizza with Radicchio and Feta, 46
Flour, 11
Flour tortillas, 32
Fontina and Gruyere Pizza Shell with Skirt Steak Salad, 108–109
Fruits
  Apple Crumble "Pizza," 119
  Apricot and Blackberry Pizza with Camembert and Sweet Ricotta Cheese, 120–121
  Grilled Strawberries and Mango Chocolate Pizza, 123
  Mixed Berries on Grilled Pizza Shell with Mascarpone Spread, 117–118

G

Garlic
  Bloody Mary Shrimp Pizza with Fried Garlic, 90–91
  Clam and Roasted Garlic Thin-Crust Pizza, 69

Garlic-Grilled Chicken and Pepperoni Pizza with Smoked Gouda, 53
  Pizza Bianca with Roasted Garlic, Ricotta, and Broccoli Rabe, 64–65
  roasted, 33
  Tenderloin and Portobello Mushroom Pizza with Roasted Garlic, 77
Gas grilling, 35–36
Goat cheese
  Grilled Asparagus and Cheese Pizza with White Truffle Oil, 56–57
  Pesto, Olive, and Goat Cheese, 99
Gorgonzola with Tarragon, Pear and, 98
Gouda cheese
  BBQ Chicken Pizza with Smoked Gouda and Grilled Pineapples, 43
  Garlic-Grilled Chicken and Pepperoni Pizza with Smoked Gouda, 53
Greek-Style Pizza, Individual Grilled, 58–59
Grilling, 35–36
Gruyere Pizza Shell with Skirt Steak Salad, Fontina and, 108–109

H

Ham, Brunch Pizza with Scrambled Eggs and Tasso, 75
Herbed Pizza Dough, 26
Herbs, 14
Hummus and Grilled Eggplant Pizza with Feta and Oven-Dried Tomatoes, 95

I

Italian sausage. see Sausage

L

Lavash pizzas, 32, 97–99
  Caramelized Onion and Rosemary with Pancetta, 99
  Pear and Gorgonzola with Tarragon, 98
  Pesto, Olive, and Goat Cheese, 99
  Prosciutto and Basil, 98
Leek and Golden Potato Grilled Pizza, Caramelized, 48

M

Mango Chocolate Pizza, Grilled Strawberries and, 123

Marinara and Mozzarella Pizza with Stuffed Crust, 92
Mascarpone cheese
Grilled Strawberries and Mango Chocolate Pizza, 123
Mixed Berries on Grilled Pizza Shell with Mascarpone Spread, 117–118
Meatballs
Meatball and Tomato Stew Grilled Pizza, 44–45
New York–Style Stone-Baked Pizza, 54–55
Mushrooms
Grilled Vegetable Salad Pizza with Balsamic Vinaigrette, 112–113
Roasted Wild Mushroom Pizza with Pancetta and Feta, 50–51
Shitake Mushroom Breakfast Pizza, 86–87
Tenderloin and Portobello Mushroom Pizza with Roasted Garlic, 77

N
Neapolitan pizza, 9, 11
No-Oil Neapolitan-Style Pizza Dough, 24
New York–Style Stone-Baked Pizza, 54–55

O
Oils, 12
Olives
Individual Grilled Greek-Style Pizza, 58–59
Pesto and Black Olive Pizza, 61
Pesto, Olive, and Goat Cheese, 99
Onion and Rosemary with Pancetta, Caramelized, 99
Oven baking, 35

P
Pancetta
Caramelized Onion and Rosemary with Pancetta, 99
Roasted Wild Mushroom Pizza with Pancetta and Feta, 50–51
Shitake Mushroom Breakfast Pizza, 86–87
Parmesan Balsamic Vinaigrette, 112–113
Pasta
Ziti Pizza with Citrus Chicken and Mozzarella, 68
Pear and Gorgonzola with Tarragon, 98

Pepperoni
Deli Counter Calzone, 67
Garlic-Grilled Chicken and Pepperoni Pizza with Smoked Gouda, 53
Peppers
Asian Salad Grilled Pizza, 115
Bloody Mary Shrimp Pizza with Fried Garlic, 90–91
Chicago-Style Deep Dish Pizza, 62
roasted, 33
Western Omelet Grilled Pizza, 76
Pesto
Basil Pesto Pizza Dough, 31
Cilantro Mint Pesto, 58–59
freezing, 21
Pesto and Black Olive Pizza, 61
Pesto, Olive, and Goat Cheese, 99
Proven Basil Pesto, 20–21
Wood-Grilled Chicken Pizza with Radicchio and Feta, 46
Pineapples, BBQ Chicken with Smoked Gouda and Grilled, 43
Pizza Bianca with Roasted Garlic, Ricotta, and Broccoli Rabe, 64–65
Pizza Margherita, 9, 39
Potatoes
Caramelized Leek and Golden Potato Grilled Pizza, 48
Pizza with Rosemary Shrimp and Spicy Golden Potatoes, 80–81
Prosciutto
Deli Counter Calzone, 67
Prosciutto and Basil, 98

R
Radicchio and Feta, Wood-Grilled Chicken Pizza with, 46
Ricotta
Apricot and Blackberry Pizza with Camembert and Sweet Ricotta Cheese, 120–121
Pizza Bianca with Roasted Garlic, Ricotta, and Broccoli Rabe, 64–65, 64–65

S
Salad pizzas, 104–115
Ancho-Seared Shrimp and Spicy Caesar Pizza, 111
Asian Salad Grilled Pizza, 115
Chicken Caesar Salad Pizza, 106–107
Fontina and Gruyere Pizza Shell with Skirt Steak Salad, 108–109
Grilled Vegetable Salad Pizza with Balsamic Vinaigrette, 112–113

Salami
Deli Counter Calzone, 67
Salmon
Pizza Montréal, 100
Sauces
Basic Tomato Sauce, 17
Béchamel Sauce, 100
Cabernet Chocolate Sauce, 123
Proven Basil Pesto, 20–21
Spicy Tomato Sauce, 19
Sauerkraut Pizza with Dark Beer Crust, German Sausage and, 93
Sausage
Chicago-Style Deep Dish Pizza, 62
Ciabatta Pizza Loaves, 88–89
German Sausage and Sauerkraut Pizza with Dark Beer Crust, 93
Meatball and Tomato Stew Grilled Pizza, 44–45
New York-Style Stone-Baked Pizza, 54–55
Western Omelet Grilled Pizza, 76
Seafood
Ancho-Seared Shrimp and Spicy Caesar Pizza, 111
Black Bean and Roasted Corn Pizza with Seared Shrimp and Monchego Cheese, 102–103
Bloody Mary Shrimp Pizza with Fried Garlic, 90–91
Clam and Roasted Garlic Thin-Crust Pizza, 69
Grilled Pizza with Fried Calamari, 101
Pizza Montréal, 100
Pizza with Rosemary Shrimp and Spicy Golden Potatoes, 80–81
Teriyaki Shrimp Grilled Pizza, 84–85
Semolina, 11
Sesame Ginger Dressing, 115
Shitake Mushroom Breakfast Pizza, 86–87
Shrimp
Ancho-Seared Shrimp and Spicy Caesar Pizza, 111
Black Bean and Roasted Corn Pizza with Seared Shrimp and Monchego Cheese, 102–103
Bloody Mary Shrimp Pizza with Fried Garlic, 90–91
Pizza with Rosemary Shrimp and Spicy Golden Potatoes, 80–81
Teriyaki Shrimp Grilled Pizza, 84–85
Spinach
Bloody Mary Shrimp Pizza with Fried Garlic, 90–91

Pizza Montréal, 100
Spinach-Stuffed Pizza, 40–41
Strawberries and Mango Chocolate Pizza, Grilled, 123
Sweet Pizza Dough, 29
Sweet pizzas
Apple Crumble "Pizza," 119
Apricot and Blackberry Pizza with Camembert and Sweet Ricotta Cheese, 120–121
Grilled Strawberries and Mango Chocolate Pizza, 123
Mixed Berries on Grilled Pizza Shell with Mascarpone Spread, 117–118

T
Tenderloin and Portobello Mushroom Pizza with Roasted Garlic, 77
Thai Chicken Pizza, 78
Tomatoes, 14
Hummus and Grilled Eggplant Pizza with Feta and Oven-Dried Tomatoes, 95
Meatball and Tomato Stew Grilled Pizza, 44–45
oven-dried, 33
Tomato sauce
basic, 17
spicy, 19
Toppings, 13–14
Tortillas, 32

V
Vegetables, 14. see also specific types
Grilled Vegetable Salad Pizza with Balsamic Vinaigrette, 112–113
Vinaigrette, Parmesan Balsamic, 112–113

W
Water, 12
Whole Wheat and Honey Pizza Dough, 25

Y
Yeast, 11–12

Z
Ziti Pizza with Citrus Chicken and Mozzarella, 68
Zucchini
Grilled Vegetable Salad Pizza with Balsamic Vinaigrette, 112–113

Acknowledgments

Behind the scenes, having spent endless hours at their computers and desks, are a number of people that made *Pizza*, my second book, possible. I thank them all. To my photographer and friend Allan Penn, and art director and friend Silke Braun, I owe immense gratitude for their artful and creative eyes. They are both truly talented individuals (not to mention patient!). I would like to thank editor Winnie Prentiss and project manager Rochelle Bourgault for their guidance and laborious task of making me look good on paper. I know deadlines are set for a reason—and that's not to miss them—thanks to Winnie for her patience. I have a large network of friends and colleagues who consistently have my best interests at heart and wish to see me succeed. Thanks to all of them: Tony, who knows I can't live without him; Steve, Erin, and Cameron; Kerri, Brian, and Sarah; Cliff and Kathy; Theresa and Joe; and my Texas partner, Randy. So much thanks to those who support me in everything I do. And, most of all, thank you to my parents, brother, and sister who always inspire me to achieve my best.

Lastly, I thank the readers who chose this book over others to indulge in—good luck in the kitchen and may every dish be a creative inspiration.

About the Author

Dwayne Ridgaway, a native of Kerrville, Texas, now lives in Bristol, Rhode Island. He is the author of the well-received *Lasagna: The Art of Layered Cooking* and a contributing author, food stylist, and recipe developer for several cooking magazines. Dwayne currently works in Rhode Island as a food and beverage consultant, caterer, and event designer. A graduate of the highly respected Johnson and Wales University, Dwayne has made a career out of exploring and celebrating the culinary arts. His passions lie in fresh ingredients and new flavors. Exploring everything the world has to offer in both techniques and flavors, Dwayne makes it his goal to combine these elements, with inspired cooking, to develop recipes that anyone can execute and enjoy. With this, his second book, Dwayne hopes home cooks everywhere will begin to explore their tastes and passions, and use his recipes and writing as groundwork for their own personal creativity.